SUBWAYLAND

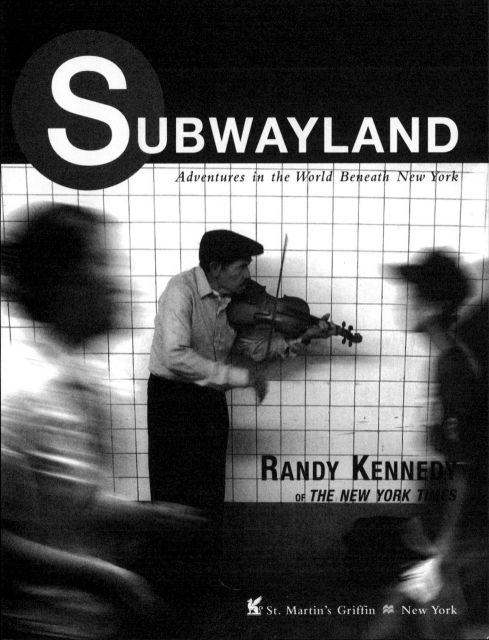

SUBWAYLAND

Adventures in the World Beneath New York

RANDY KENNEDY
OF *THE NEW YORK TIMES*

St. Martin's Griffin ≈ New York

6-29-2004
GBG
$ 13.95

www.stmartins.com

Designed by Susan Yang

Library of Congress Cataloging-in-Publication Data

Kennedy, Randy.
    Subwayland: adventures in the world beneath New York / Randy Kennedy.
        p. cm.
   ISBN 0-312-32434-0
   EAN 978-0312-32434-6
   1. New York (N.Y.)—Description and travel. 2. Subways—New York
(State)—New York. 3. New York (N.Y.)—Social life and customs.
4. New York (N.Y.)—Biography. I. New York times. II. Title.

F128.55K46 2004
917.47'10443—dc22   200306054

10 9 8 7 6 5 4 3

For my mother. And my father, who always loved a good story.

CONTENTS

ACKNOWLEDGMENTS

Gratitude for this book is owed to more people than I can possibly mention. First to Jon Landman, whose enthusiasm supplied it with energy. To Janet Krone Kennedy, my wife, for love, support, proofreading and a deep reserve of subway complaints that led to many good columns. To dozens of friends, relatives, Times *colleagues and other resources of ideas and inspiration, among them Paul, my brother, Ann and Ron Krone, Larry Krone, Erin St. John Kelly, Charles von Simson, Chris Tatti, Regina McLean, Sarah Kershaw, Lynette Holloway, Christine Kay, Wendell Jamieson, Joe Sexton, Gerry Mullany, Patrick LaForge, Jim Dwyer, Eden Ross Lipson, Savannah Walker, Susan Chira, Ethan Friedman, David Pirmann, Richard Abate, Roxanne Robertson and Gene Russianoff. Finally, to many at the Metropolitan Transportation Authority, New York City Transit, and the Transport Workers Union, Local 100, including Al O'Leary, Tom Kelly, Paul Fleuranges, Charles Seaton, Deirdre Parker, Ed Watt and John Samuelsen.*

INTRODUCTION

Togetherness, circa 1960

"The people are growing to like the Subway method of transit, and the growth of their liking, great and measurable as it is, has only begun."

—Edward P. Bryan, vice president of the
Interborough Rapid Transit Company, January 1905

A century ago this year, New York City gave birth to a subway, and the subway gave a multitude of gifts in return.

The most practical were the powers of speed and sprawl—just 15 minutes from City Hall to Harlem; just 40 years from the bottom of Brooklyn to the top of the Bronx, with stations scattered like seed-corn in between. Wherever New Yorkers took the subway, the city rode along.

In the process, the subway gave us much more than a way to work and back home. It gave us an object of pride and fascination, fear and loathing. It gave us a permanent topic of conversation and a perfect excuse for being late. It gave poets a new muse and moviemakers a new set. It gave warmth to the cold, a bed to the weary and a captive audience to anyone with a cheap guitar.

But it also gave another gift, much less appreciated and more important, one that changed the city fundamentally and forever: the gift of proximity.

In other words, the subway made us sit together.

And stand together. And, of course, wait and sweat and swear together. If you are reading this while riding a Lexington Avenue express train with someone's shoulder blade pressed into your left eye socket, you will think it is a very bad joke. At this moment, in fact, you are probably longing to live in a place—meaning basically any other place in the country—where most people go places inside the upholstered cocoons of their cars, catching glimpses of their fellow citizens through safety glass at 70 miles an hour.

Yet bitter as it may be, proximity has powerful medicinal qualities. It might not perform miracles. It might not make New Yorkers talk or smile more or even be particularly more personable, but inside hundreds of train cars coursing at any minute above and below the streets, it is nonetheless weaving sturdy threads through the fabric of the city.

Every day, subway riders find themselves inches from people with whom they would not willingly choose to share a long city block. But like schoolchildren in detention, riders form a kind of unspoken bond while forced into each others' company—call it the kinship of the mildly oppressed. The busboy and the bond broker, sitting haunch to haunch, are sitting there for the same reason: The train they are riding is generally the fastest and most efficient way to get where they are going. If it succeeds in this regard or even if it fails them (in fact, especially if it fails), the two share something—surely the only thing they will ever share—until the doors open and they step out.

Statistics show that in the waning years of the 20th century, six out of every 10 people traveling toward the center of Manhattan on an average workday morning traveled there inside a subway car. This is a level of enforced neighborhood not found anywhere else in America, even in Chicago with its El or Boston with its T. And it has done a great deal to make New York—always an odd appendage to the rest of the nation—a true American anomaly, more tolerant and cohesive than a city its size ever had a right to be.

In the first year of the subway's operations, there were firsts of many things now considered inseparable from life in New York City. There were the first complaints about the heat, about the quality of the air, about germs, about noise and about delays (on the first full day of operation, express service failed twice because of electrical problems). There were also the first complaints about crowding, perverts and lousy announcements. (An editorial in the Times put it this way: "If any one form of words is better calculated than another to implant a homicidal impulse in the breast of the average man, it is the formula 'Step Lively!' which has gained a new vogue through its employment by the trainmen of the Subway system.")

In the first year, the system was hobbled by the first transit strike and the first power failure. Trains were delayed for the first time by a water-main break, a fire, a stray dog. The first subway worker was killed by a train. The first passenger was crushed to death between the train and the platform. The first person was struck and killed by a speeding train (an unfortunate resident of the Bronx named Leidschnudel Dreispul). The first fatal crash of two subway trains also occurred (it was at the 23rd Street station; William H. Curran, a 17-year-old law clerk, died afterward).

The first movie was made in the subway (a documentary for August Belmont, the system's chief financier) and the first play was written about the subway (the plot concerned a scheme in which unsatisfied husbands killed their wives by throwing them onto the tracks).

The first bar named for the subway was in operation (the Subway Tavern at Bleecker and Broome). New Yorkers took the subway for the first time to a ball game (the New York Highlanders, later to become the Yankees, beat the Washington Senators, 5 to 3, at American League Park in Washington Heights on April 22, 1905). New Yorkers also took their first trip by subway to the first New Year's celebration in Times Square (before 1904, the biggest crowds usually gathered near Trinity Church).

Finally, the first known proposal of marriage in the subway was made and accepted. (William Darbeau, firefighter, popped the question to Miss Helen Dodd, newsgirl, at Bleecker Street. She said she had to check with her mother first.)

Over the last two and a half years, while writing a weekly column about the subway, I have ridden it from one end to the other more times than I can remember. I have been to almost all of its 468 stations. I've spent nights aboard it. I've interrupted readers to ask them what they were reading, and I've wakened nappers to ask them what they were dreaming. I've walked along the tracks, waded through the waters, savored the smells and once—though I was sworn never to reveal where or when—I climbed into a motorman's cab and drove a train. In the course of my reporting, I've also ridden in close proximity with many of the subway's most interesting riders, including the mayor of New York City, a South American magician and a group of mangy pigeons from Far Rockaway.

For a newspaper reporter, it is a beat that is very hard to beat. About what other single subject could one write and include (albeit sometimes unwisely, because of bad deadline pressure) mention of Dante, Dr. Seuss, "West Side Story," Arthur Miller, Jennifer Holliday, the city of Bombay, the width of a bass boat, Michaelangelo, Mount Everest, Mount Rushmore, Ethel Merman, Sigmund Freud, Salvador Dali, Tito Puente, Terry Southern and Count von Count from "Sesame Street"?

After spending so much time in the subway, I can tell you that a funny thing happens when you lock millions of people together underground in oblong metal rooms for a certain period of time. It creates a place that is much more than the sum of its parts. In fact, it generates a society unto itself, with its own citizenry,

INTRODUCTION

government, flora and fauna, customs, myths, taboos, tragedies and secret histories.

Tourists and occasional visitors have always described it that way, as a strange and slightly perilous place they explored while in New York City. But even veteran riders regard it as essentially foreign territory. We wonder why things work the way they do in the subway. We talk of the bizarre ways people behave there. We tell of the guy we saw there with the python draped around his neck. (Someone we tell will have seen him, too.) We tell horror stories and funny stories and sob stories that are better because they originated there. Why is it that a bad saxophone player sounds a little more talented playing on a crowded platform? Why is it that the Chinese violinist I heard at Times Square one July day playing "Jingle Bells" got more laughs there than he would have on the street above? It is because the subway, while inseparable from the city, is also a world apart from it. For that reason, I've tried to arrange the following columns as a travelogue, the notes of an explorer within his own city, unequal parts sociology, anthropology, zoology, theology and biology, with a little pathology thrown in for good measure.

As I write this, I am taking notes again, on a Q express train bound from downtown Brooklyn to midtown Manhattan. Technically, I am not exploring this time. I am just going to work, the way I always go—Union Street to DeKalb to Canal to Union Square to 34th Street to that great cauldron called Times Square. In the middle of this trip is my favorite part—the Manhattan Bridge—the homely, hardworking sister of the Brooklyn, which I can see out the left window on this summer day, resplendent but subwayless, as my train levitates over the East River and threads itself into the city. I am in the second car from the front, my usual berth because it puts me out in Times Square at the foot of a staircase that forms part of a carefully planned escape route from that overcrowded station, a route I've taken so many times it often surprises me not to see my footprints worn into the floor.

I was raised in a farming town in West Texas called Plains, population about 1,400, where my abiding desire as a teenager was to live any place where I would be able to walk out the front door and see people I didn't know. My train car this morning, in fact every car I take every morning, fulfills that requirement quite well. It is 9:45. There are about 80 people in here with me, half of them standing, as I am. I know none of them, except one woman seated behind me in the corner, whom I recognize from work. We make eye contact but come to that immediate wordless understanding that acquaintances and sometimes even spouses reach on morning subway trips. She wants to read her newspaper; I want to write in my notebook. We agree to ignore each other. This is fine. (In other cities, people go to work alone, with their thoughts and their car radios. For most, it is the only private time of the day. The subway serves the same purpose, except that New Yorkers must seek their privacy in the most public place imaginable—along with a million others seeking the same thing.)

In the car with me this morning is the usual mix of the mundane and the subtly marvelous that constitute the land of the subway. A few feet away, a seated man with long sideburns is about halfway through a dog-eared paperback of "Lawrence of Arabia." On one side of him is a small man reading the sports pages of a Chinese newspaper. On the other side is another small man reading an article about the Rev. Al Sharpton in a Russian newspaper. Across from them is a tall elderly man wearing a felt yarmulke and fancy running shoes, hunched intently over a Hebrew prayer book. The only person I can hear talking in the entire car is a skinny teenager in a Knicks jersey, hitting on a woman in a flower-print skirt, both of them crowded near a door. He's saying to her, "You ain't *heard* me sing yet," and she's smiling. Seated inches away but oblivious to this conversation because of his headphones is a man wearing black sunglasses, black jeans and a black T-shirt with the words "No, I will not fix your computer" written across his chest.

Further up, a woman with long black hair is scooping it behind her ears and beginning to apply her makeup methodically with a small compact mirror. Over the bridge she is brushing on rouge. By Canal Street she has moved to eyeliner, penciled on carefully between lurches. By Union Square it is lip liner and between 23rd and 28th lipstick the color of a city fire truck. Meanwhile, the man reading "Lawrence of Arabia" has laid it on his lap. His reading companions have departed, and he is trying to sleep but managing only the thousand-yard subway stare, the kind seen on the faces in the hidden-camera photographs Walker Evans took aboard the trains in the late 1930's. I finally get off at Times Square, just behind the man who will not fix my computer, the praying man and the skinny Don Juan, whose object of affection seems to have disappeared somewhere along the way.

A calculation occurred to me as I watched my fellow riders that morning. If a New Yorker averages half an hour on the subway every day over the course of his or her adult life, say 50 years, this adds up to slightly more than a *year* spent in the subway. It adds up, in other words, to a whole lot of life being lived down there. And it helps explain why the subway has played so many roles in the life of its city over the last century. Besides being the people's limousine, it has been, by turns, a lunchroom, a library, a dormitory, a chapel, a concert hall, a bazaar, a Bowery mission and a boudoir. It has served as a deathbed and, many times, a maternity ward for babies who could not wait until the next stop. It has been the city's biggest singles scene and its biggest station wagon. Sometimes, late on weekend nights, it smells like a saloon. Early in the 21st century, it is now officially impossible to imagine this city without it.

The first time my parents visited New York, in the early 90's, I was a little nervous about taking them on the train. I decided that we would start out at the Court Street station in Brooklyn Heights, near my apartment, because it was relatively nice-looking and clean, a gentle introduction. But as soon as the elevator doors parted on the mezzanine, we found ourselves in very close proximity to a very large man who was calmly relieving himself in a corner. I felt my mother stiffen. I think my dad grinned. I was horrified at first. But then, as we hurried past the man and his puddle, I thought: What better introduction to a place where you can see anything?

After three years of writing this column, I sometimes feel as if I've seen everything there is to see in the subway. Thankfully, I'm proven wrong every day.

CITIZENS OF THE SUBWAY

The last great democracy: On the subway, the mayor is just another man in search of a seat.

SMITTEN BY THE SUBWAY

If you have set foot on a subway platform during the last 20 years, there is a decent chance that he has been standing there next to you, a small, smiling man in no hurry to catch a train.

He was probably carrying a green satchel with a tiny American flag stitched on the flap. From this satchel, he probably produced a pair of junk-store binoculars or a camera and pointed one in the direction of a rust-stained wall that seemed to warrant neither close inspection nor documentation.

You probably did not notice him. He tends to fade into the tile-work. And that is how Philip Ashforth Coppola of Maplewood, N.J., likes it. But once, on August 29, 1978, he pinned a plastic envelope to his shirt, slipped a name tag inside and summoned up the courage to conduct his own private poll at four Midtown subway stations. As he later wrote, he "collared whoever looked like a likely candidate," and with all the intensity of the Ancient Mariner, he asked a question:

"Are you aware of the subway art?"

The art to which Mr. Coppola referred was the art that he loves most in the world, the masterpieces in mosaic, faience, terra cotta, tile and steel that a grander generation of public builders bequeathed the humble and hurried subway rider.

That summer morning, his questions elicited mostly ignorance and indifference. But the subject mattered dearly to Mr. Coppola for a couple of reasons. One was that so many of his beloved treasures were either crumbling or being blithely entombed in subway renovations.

Another reason was that Mr. Coppola, then on the verge of turning 30, a sometime dishwasher, sometime printing press operator with little training in design and none in writing, had just decided to devote the rest of his life to writing and publishing at his own expense an exhaustive, multivolume, painstakingly detailed history of the design and decoration of every one of the stations—496, by his count—that ever existed in the subway system.

In the pantheon of the New York City subway buff, a loose fraternity of urban transit fans who range from simple romantics to near-maniacs, you could think of Mr. Coppola as the obsessive's obsessive.

He does not, like one buff in Sheepshead Bay, Brooklyn, have a mock-up of a motorman's cab in his bedroom, supplemented with recorded sounds from the subway to make sitting in the cab feel more authentic.

He does not, like another buff in Fort Greene, Brooklyn, live in an apartment that has been converted into a miniature subway system, full of expensive handmade model trains.

He certainly does not, like one veteran buff who turns up at Transit Authority functions, sport a large tattoo of a subway car on his bicep.

But what Mr. Coppola has done takes him far beyond the bounds of even the most devoted railroad hobbyist. For a quarter of a century, he has spent nearly every spare minute of his life—weekends, vacations, long nights too many to count—haunting subway stations, libraries, archives, museums and creaky microfilm readers in search of even the tiniest shards of fact for his masterwork.

He could have ended up another Joe Gould, the Greenwich Village eccentric who claimed to have written a nine-million-word opus called "The Oral History of Our Time," largely drawn from overheard conversations and, in the end, largely existing only in Mr. Gould's imagination.

But Mr. Coppola was not just a dreamer. In 1984, after almost six years of hovering over his sketch pad and his I.B.M. Selectric II, he self-published the first heavy volume of "Silver Connections: A Fresh Perspective on the New York Area Subway Systems." Another volume appeared in 1990 and a third in 1994. The fourth and most recent, a thick digression that covers the design of the old Manhattan and Hudson Railroad, came out in 1999. And after revising the first volume ("Simply far too much purple prose in that one," he says, warning, "Do not read too deeply into it.") he plans to begin No. 5, which he hopes will appear in 2004 and take the subway saga all the way up to 1915. Through the years, he even built a readership, including the artist Roy Lichtenstein, who consulted the volumes when making the subway mural that now hangs in Times Square.

Stacked on top of one another, the volumes, published in small batches, measure nine inches. Not counting the mind-boggling bibliographies and indexes, they add up to more than 1,900 pages, several hundred thousand words and more than one thousand of Mr. Coppola's hand drawings.

Mr. Coppola is now 52 years old.

He has 404 more subway stations to go.

"I always thought nine was a good round number, nine volumes," he says. "Now I am not so sure."

He hopes his readers will like his volumes, of course. But you get the sneaking sense from Mr. Coppola that his most devoted reader will always be Philip Ashforth Coppola.

"Now if you're not the sort to be terribly concerned about whence there came the New York subway, nor how it came about," he writes in the introduction to Volume I, "then I still suggest you keep this book on your bedside table, in case you can't sleep some night; I especially recommend my thoughts upon the extensions to the upper Broadway stations, found in my review of the 137th Street IRT station (pp. 338-341).

"A paragraph or two," he adds, "should send you off splendidly."

To outsiders, the world of Mr. Coppola, the world of the true subway buff, or rail fan, as many like to be called, has never been easy to visit.

On some level, of course, every New Yorker has felt the fascination. The subway has always meant a lot more to the city than just a way to get around. As much as the Statue of Liberty or the Empire State Building, it has represented the monumental ambition of the city itself. It has also been one of the best methods for veteran New Yorkers to travel back in time, to the old neighborhood, to the transit gloria of Ebbets Field, to that rite of passage when they were finally old enough to ride by themselves.

Many buffs approach the subway as pure sentimentalists, drawn to the subject by a mixture of nostalgia and municipal pride. These are the buffs who know the map so well they don't have to look at it, the ones who like to stare out the front windows of trains, who still argue about the relative merits of the IRT over the BMT in an age when few commuters know what the letters ever meant. (The Interborough Rapid Transit system is now the numbered lines, and the Brooklyn–Manhattan Transit system is part of the lettered lines.)

These are buffs like Stan Fischler, who has written four books on New York subways and trolleys. His favorite facts are the purely personal ones, such as how the old BMT "standard" cars had a jump seat that folded down so that a 5-year-old Stan could stand on it and stick his head out the front window. Or how the old trains on the Brighton Line, as they passed the curve at Beverly Road, used to bang out a rhythm that sounded exactly like the drumbeat in Benny Goodman's "China Boy."

"When I first found out it was a nickel," said Mr. Fischler, "I said to myself, 'Oh my *God,* I'd pay five bucks for something like this, easy.' For a kid, it was paradise."

But the subway also tends to take its votaries to levels of fascination where most people find the air too thin.

In many ways, of course, they are no different from any other hardcore buffs: Trekkies, Civil War re-enactors, J. F. K. assassination buffs who come to blows over the role of the umbrella man in Dealey Plaza.

But while the lure of those subjects is somewhat apparent, it is not as easy to figure out what motivates the dedicated rail fan.

One of the telltale signs is that he—it is nearly always a he; most rail fans are male, middle-aged and single; the married ones call their wives "rail widows"—can sit for several hours watching stunningly prosaic slides of subway trains that, to the untrained eye, all look pretty much identical.

But for the buff, a train picture holds the same appeal that a pinned butterfly holds for a lepidopterist. At an early summer meeting of the New York chapter of the Electric Railroaders' Association, a club formed in the early 1950's, about two hundred people filled an auditorium at the College of Insurance in Lower Manhattan to see the work of Harold Pinsker, a popular amateur train photographer, who presented what the program called "a mix of his best slides from the 1980's."

The textbook train-buff photograph is known as a roster shot. To the outsider, one thing becomes apparent immediately about roster shots: there are no people in them. The aim is to show trains and only trains, with no passengers to block the view or scenery to distract the eye. (An Internet guide on taking roster shots counsels: "The main idea is to portray the locomotive in a very realistic and straightforward manner. Leave your artistic ambitions at home.")

An authentic rail fan also devotes as much of his vacation as possible to riding on and taking roster shots of subways around the world. While Mr. Pinsker's slides flashed on the screen that night, Charlie Akins, the longtime president of the rail club, whispered about his coming vacation to Budapest, where he would spend a week checking out Hungarian subways with a group of fans from around the United States.

Mr. Akins, 54, a manager for the Social Security Administration, has also vacationed on subways in Hong Kong, London, Paris, Montreal and every American city that has one. (A rail-fan vacation guide warns about the pitfalls of taking nonfans on such trips: "If you want to be accompanied trackside by a spouse, child or buddy who doesn't like trains, in an attempt to enlighten them as to the mystique of the rails, then by all means do so. But be forewarned, you do so at your own peril.")

Truth be told, even people who consider themselves fine amateur subway buffs probably could not handle it.

"Let's put it this way," said Gene Russianoff, a lawyer for the Straphangers Campaign, the riders' advocacy group. "Transit advocates are from Mars and transit buffs are from Venus. They're really two completely different types of people."

"I just can't sit there and hear about which cars are married pairs and which used a certain kind of lug nut," said Mr. Russianoff, who has been an advocate and subway expert for more than two decades.

Over the years, the unusual ardor of rail fans has given rise to a long list of less-than-flattering nicknames. The most widely used term is *foamer*, which may have been used first by Amtrak employees to refer to rail fans who grew so excited when looking at trains they seemed to be rabid. Another theory holds that this term was adapted from the acronym FOMITE, which stood for "fanatically obnoxious mentally incompetent train enthusiast."

Other names include *glazer* (eyes glaze over at sight of trains); *gerf* (glassy-eyed rail fan); and *flim* (foamer living with mother.) Transit Authority employees privately use a much stronger term: *fern*, in which the "r" and the "n" stand for "rail nut" and the "f" stands for what you think it stands for.

Many Transit Authority officials hold so dim a view of rail fans, in fact, that they do not like to comment publicly about them for fear that it will only encourage the more unstable, some of whom, officials complain, trespass into rail yards and risk life and limb to get pictures of trains.

There are even a few who cross the line into real criminality— fans who love trains so much that they feel compelled to take them.

Darius McCollum, probably the best known, began at 15, persuading a motorman to let him drive an E train. Over the years, he frequently impersonated Transit Authority employees, commandeered buses and, once, sneaked into a control tower at 57th Street and tripped the emergency brakes on an N train.

"There are people who are interested in subways, and then there are people who are crazy," one transit official said. "They tend to show up at any event where we're rolling out new equipment or making any changes in the system. You always know who it's going to be. And they don't look like regular human beings."

Rail fans hate it when the term *subway buff* is used in newspapers to describe someone who decides to steal a train. "Guys who do that are not rail fans," said David Pirmann, a buff who maintains one of the best Internet collections of New York subway history, lore and facts (www.nycsubway.org). "Guys who do that are crackpots and vandals, and they should be locked up for a long time."

In their defense, buffs point out that if it were not for buffs, many of whom are or have been New York Transit employees, many pieces of history now in the authority's Transit Museum in downtown Brooklyn probably would have ended up in a metal shredder. In his book, "The Subway," Mr. Fischler relates the story of Frank Turdik, a transit employee who, in the mid-1960's, took several old cars that were about to be scrapped and hid them in an unused tunnel. The cars were preserved and are still around today, rolled out by the Transit Museum for special events.

"A lot of people ask me how I can be so into this," said Mr. Pirmann, a systems management consultant in Manhattan. "And I say: 'Look, it's a hobby. I mean, my parents collect little glass shoes. They must have seven hundred of them. This is what I do. You might think it's crazy, but I think it's cool.'"

The birth of the subway and of the subway buff were roughly coincident. But the obsession gathered speed when the Transit Authority began to scrap many of the first subway cars after World War II.

No one really knows how many serious buffs are out there now. The Electric Railroaders' Association has about 650 members in the city. Mr. Akins, the president, says a striking change over the years has been the growth in the number of members who are transit employees, apparently more emboldened now to admit that the subway is their passion as well as their job. The next largest club in the city, the New York Railroad Enthusiasts, whose interests extend to steam and diesel trains, has about 150 members. But there are thousands more buffs who are simply not joiners and will never be counted. They are scattered throughout the city, the country and the world, nurturing their fascination in solitude.

One such buff is Derek Nisbett, an intensive case manager for the state's Office of Mental Health. Mr. Nisbett, 44, is the man who has bought more than one hundred scale-model brass and plastic subway cars, costing about $500 each, and has been slowly turning his Fort Greene studio apartment into a miniature subway system. The crown jewel will be a set of elevated tracks that will circle his bed. "I collect only subway trains," he said. "Everybody who knows me knows that."

Another is Paul Kronenberg, 56, a math tutor in Sheepshead Bay. He is the man who has built the eerily realistic mock-up of a motorman's cab in his bedroom from old IND train parts. He said the idea came to him when he was working near a Coney Island subway scrap yard in the 1970's.

"Originally I just wanted the controller from a cab," Mr. Kronenberg said. "Then I bought a brake stand, a door, a windshield, the brake boxes, the motorman's seat, a pressure gauge." He built the walls out of particle board and painted them the exact gray-green color of the old trains by mixing Sears paint with pigment.

"Someone I knew saw it, and he said, 'When you drop dead and the authorities come in here and see this thing, you're going to make the newspapers,'" he said. "And I just kind of freaked out when he said that. But most people who know me don't think it's all that strange. They know I don't take it all that seriously."

Arguably the most isolated subway buff of all is a man named Michael Vincze. He is not, however, a loner by choice. He is incarcerated in South Woods State Prison in Bridgeton, N.J., where he dreams about the Polo Grounds shuttle of his youth and has built a substantial library of subway books in his cell. He is such a devoted collector, in fact, that he has bought all four volumes of Mr. Coppola's "Silver Connections," and, like many of Mr. Coppola's fans from New York to Texas to Minnesota to Maryland, the inmate has kept up a correspondence with the author for a decade, even while being transferred from prison to prison.

"I really don't know much about him," Mr. Coppola said the other day. "I've never asked him why he's in prison. From what I can tell he has a fine mind and a nice personality. He knows a lot about the story of the subways."

Mr. Coppola wants desperately to tell him, and everyone else who is interested, the rest of the subway's story, if only he can find time to tell it, between his job as a printing press operator and the care of his 90-year-old mother, Mary, with whom he has lived since his father, Joseph, died in 1974.

The other day, wandering the empty, cathedral-like Chambers Street station on the J line, one of his favorites, he was asked to explain why he loves the New York City subway so much, enough to devote his life to it.

After all, he has spent nearly all his life in Maplewood, nowhere near a subway station. He never dreamed of growing up to be a motorman or a conductor. His father, who worked on Wall Street, hated the subway and avoided it whenever possible.

"Why did I pick the subways?" Mr. Coppola says, pondering for a long time. "Oh Lordy, that's a good one. I guess I felt like it needed a little public relations work, that's all."

"I thought it needed a voice," he said. "And then I just got hooked."

Maybe a better way of saying this can be found in the hand-written inscription for Volume III of Mr. Coppola's life's work. Quoting from the Book of Luke, it says: "For where your treasure is, there will your heart be also."

Mr. Coppola certainly hopes that this is a true statement. At his current rate of publication, he figures he will finish his subway history at some point in his late 80's.

—ORIGINALLY PUBLISHED JULY 23, 2000

THEY STAND FOR CHANGE

On the bright side, you could think of it this way: John Del Signore and Victor Cretella are victims of their own success.

About a year and a half ago, not long after Mr. Del Signore lost his job as Santa Claus at Saks Fifth Avenue, he and his friend Mr. Cretella, an independent filmmaker, decided to strike out in a slightly new direction, career-wise.

They painted their faces silver. They squeezed into silver spandex suits. They thought up a silvery name for themselves: the Mercury Men. And they went down into the subway to work.

Silver people, apparently, work by doing pretty much nothing.

But this is not as easy as it sounds. The two men's performance involves them acting like mannequins, on milk crates, for hours at a stretch without moving a muscle, without so much as blinking. The only time they spring briefly into action is when someone plunks a coin into their bucket—oil, of a sort, for the rusted joints of these tin woodsmen. Mr. Cretella, 24, will bow, with robotic stiffness. Mr. Del Signore, 25, will smile and say, "Thank you," and gesture like an android Noël Coward at an android cocktail party. And then the Mercury Men will freeze in place again.

Maybe it is something about silence and stillness in a place that is so loud and frantic. Maybe it is something about potential energy, about expectation, about the quality of subway entertainment in general. But when Mr. Cretella and Mr. Del Signore get up on their milk crates, crowds gather and people are transfixed.

They stop midstride and stare, with their mouths open. They laugh and point and take pictures and talk to complete strangers about what the two silver men are trying to tell us with their tranquillity.

"I think you guys are, like, beautiful," said a woman in pink sunglasses who passed Friday at the Times Square station and blew a kiss.

But at least one group of subway denizens seems to have decided that the Mercury Men are not beautiful or entertaining or even particularly tolerable: the police. A few weeks ago, Mr. Del Signore was handed a $50 summons for "obstructing passenger flow" in Times Square. Five days later, Mr. Cretella was also fined $50, in the same station, for "obstructing ped. traffic."

The tickets came, they said, after months in which the police at several subway stations seemed to take an increasingly dim view of their act, ordering them to move along, accusing them of panhandling and making disparaging remarks about mimes, which they are not, exactly.

They seem, they said, to have become the faces on the wanted posters for a new kind of crime in an overcrowded city: making it hard for people to walk. But others also do this—construction companies, film crews, other subway performers who are much louder and more disruptive—and the penalties seem to be handed out arbitrarily, Mr. Cretella said.

"MTV can draw a crowd on Broadway that cuts off the whole sidewalk and nobody does anything because they're Viacom and they have the money and the power to get away with that, right?"

It is not, of course, the first time the two men have had to deal with critics. "People have punched me, they've smacked me, they've poked me in the eyes, they've thrown things at me," Mr. Cretella said. "They've pretended they're going to urinate on me."

Mr. Del Signore, who usually wears a polyester tuxedo over his spandex, has had people take his pants down while he tried to stay still. He has had people pinch his rear end. Once, a man swung a tire chain at his head. Once, he chased and tackled a man who had punched him twice in the arm.

"You're silver and you've got to stand still," he explained. "Basically, you're a target."

Last Friday in Times Square, the crowd watching the two men, more than 50 people at times, was very respectful. But even so:

"Ooh, scary mimes," said one woman, hurrying past.

"Mommy, why are they there?" asked a little girl, eyes wide.

"Get a job," yelled an elderly man carrying a briefcase.

Then, just before 5 p.m., two police officers joined the crowd and one began to write something in his ticket book as the crowd looked at him with stony faces. Finally, he walked over to the two men and said, "Rush hour, guys. You got to move along."

The men now say they have decided to move along for good. "It's just too much of a risk," Mr. Del Signore said. "We never know if we're going to get a ticket, and $50 is basically a whole day's work."

Where will they go next? Sleepier stations in Brooklyn and Lower Manhattan, probably. Maybe a national "tour," in a few months. "I can see us standing in front of the Grand Canyon," Mr. Cretella said, "going to strip malls, that kind of thing."

This fall, they said, they even plan to throw their milk crates into the mayoral race, to try to make New York City more tolerant of silver men.

Their slogan? "We stand for change."

—ORIGINALLY PUBLISHED APRIL 3, 2001

THE OLD NO. 2 TRAIN TRICK

It seemed as if Olmedini, El Mago Magnifico, had performed his final trick and disappeared like the Third Avenue El.

This reporter found him for the first time about five years ago aboard an R train, changing a red scarf into a white dove. In the process, he was changing something much harder to change: a whole subway car full of sour-faced commuters turned into children again, at least for a few minutes, as they rumbled under the East River.

"The biggest trick," Olmedini likes to say, "is pulling people out of their daydreams."

When the reporter tried to find him again last winter, he began to fear that Olmedini himself had been just a daydream. He looked on the R train, with no luck. A call went out to the International Brotherhood of Magicians, who knew Olmedini. They said he was originally from Ecuador and was the only magician they knew who performed on the subway. But when they tried his number in Queens, no one answered.

They suggested calling Reuben's restaurant at Madison Avenue and 38th Street, a magician's haunt. But no one had seen him there for a while, either.

Then, last week, on a whim, his number was dialed again. And like the spring, it seemed, Olmedini had returned.

"I am sorry," he said, in richly accented Spanish, sounding like an Ecuadorean Vincent Price. "I took some time off. I did not know you were looking for me."

"Let us meet on the subway," he said.

So it was that last Friday was spent on the No. 2 train watching dollar bills float in midair, watching the bills become doves. Most of all, the day was spent watching people—even those who tried hard to feign indifference—watch Olmedini.

It is impressive enough to hear someone play a saxophone on a loud, lurching subway car. It is amazing to watch a troupe of young dancers performing a routine, complete with somersaults, down the middle of a crowded train. But to see a man on the subway produce a live, fat rabbit from an empty wooden box just inches from your eyes is something else altogether.

"That man should be in the news," said Kenneth Chrysostome, 11, whose class was on its way from Flatbush to Carnegie Hall to hear a Dvorak symphony and caught Olmedini's act between

Chambers and 14th Streets. "That man should be on the front page."

In fact, Olmedini—born Olmedo Renteria and raised in Guayaquil, Ecuador—was in the newspapers quite often in his home country. He found magic by way of the circus, which he joined at 18 to work as a booking agent. But he soon fell under the spell of a circus magician named Memper, who took the young man under his cape, showed him a handful of tricks and helped him find a job with a circus, a job that paid exactly nothing.

"They said that when I learned enough to be a real magician, then they would pay me," he recalls.

He learned to be a real magician, a very good one. But the pay never quite followed. Though Olmedini (his stage name is an homage to Houdini) became quite well known in Ecuador, levitating beautiful young assistants and transforming them into Dobermans, he could never support himself and his family the way he wanted.

So in 1988, he decided to move to New York. But the nightclub invitations did not come pouring in here, either. And so one bitter December day in 1989, when he was performing outside near Columbus Circle and the wind was making his hands go numb, he decided to go underground.

He did O.K. on the subway platforms. He later found, though, that he could do much better inside the train, where he had a captive audience and more time to collect money from appreciative viewers. So he shortened his act and built himself a sort of rolling Dr. Caligari's cabinet, using drapery fabric and wheels salvaged from baby carriages.

That was seven years ago, and he has been performing on the trains ever since, making as much as $25 an hour on good days, enough to pay his rent in Jackson Heights and send a little money back to Ecuador to help put his daughter through college.

"In the subway," he says, "I am famous."

Last Friday, he was on stage along one of his favorite routes, the No. 2 between Chambers Street and Times Square. (He has determined that the No. 2, the A, the D and the N are the most lucrative trains, and he sticks to them unwaveringly. He will let a parade of No. 3 trains pass to catch a No. 2.)

Because Olmedini, 60, still struggles with English, he does not speak a word during his brief shows but instead smiles and whistles quietly to draw people's attention, like a mass-transit Harpo Marx. After his last trick, he produces a purple banner from a seemingly empty velvet sack. He holds it up to show the bright yellow words, which say, "Thank You."

"Some performers on the trains are needy and demanding, and they're always invading my space," said Laura Meagher, a performance artist who caught his act. "With him, I just heard this whistling. And then I look up and there's a dollar floating in the air."

The life of the city's subway magician is mostly a lonely one. He lives by himself, with six doves and his rabbit, named El Cielo, which means sky, so named because his eyes are a bright blue. But his neighbors complain about the noise the doves make. And Olmedini can't become too attached to El Cielo because, like all his rabbits, he will grow too fat for his special magic box in about another year and have to be given to a pet shop.

"In my career, I have known probably more than five hundred rabbits," he says, adding, "Sometimes, I would like to stop using rabbits."

Sometimes, he adds, he would also like to stop taking the subway.

"People in the subway, they love me," he says. "But you know what my fondest wish is? It's to be so successful that I never have to work in the subway again."

—ORIGINALLY PUBLISHED MAY 29, 2001

TIMES SQUARE SHUTTLE BLUES

As stages for musical performance go, it could not be much worse. The acoustics stink. The lighting lacks all subtlety. The stage itself lists from side to side. Occasionally, the patrons smell. And every few minutes, someone interrupts to say something semi-intelligible about the Port Authority.

Even in a city where creativity can flourish in every crevice, there should be a better crevice. Yet something seems to keep bringing Brian Homa back to the Times Square shuttle, carrying a Takamine guitar, a shiny metal pot for collecting his paycheck and a mental playlist that includes everything from "The Tootsie Roll Song" to "The Star-Spangled Banner."

It may be that, coming from a place as small as Port Crane, N.Y., near Binghamton, Mr. Homa feels more comfortable performing aboard the smallest subway line in the system, oscillating back and forth under Midtown like a metronome. It may also be the particular kind of masochism practiced by people who come to New York and want it to be hard and merciless, a corrective to the comfortable place they came from.

But whatever the reason—even Mr. Homa can't quite explain it—he has made a shuttle car his only cabaret for almost three years now. And somewhere along the thousands of miles he has traveled between the Times Square and Grand Central subway stations, he has made himself one of the better known performers in the system. (The jokes about him going nowhere fast are actually funny now, he says.)

If you are a regular performer on other, more expansive lines, there's a good chance that subway riders could go weeks or even months without seeing you. But on a line as compact as the shuttle, tens of thousands of regular riders have to try very hard to miss Mr. Homa. Plus, there's no competition to speak of.

"There's one other guy named Jazz, who plays the flute," Mr. Homa said yesterday, uncasing his guitar and preparing to punch in. "He's been playing about a year longer than I have, so I give him the respect he deserves."

To spend a few mornings with Mr. Homa, 25, is to experience an intensely concentrated version of what it is like to be a subway performer. It is to see, first of all, how the depressed economy has depressed them. When Mr. Homa began playing in the summer of 1999, after moving to New York that winter, he could sometimes make more than $200 a day, his car filled with New Economy largesse. His earnings paid the rent at his Harlem apartment. Best of all, he could play his own eccentric compositions instead of pounding out Beatles covers.

"There was a while there when I really felt like I could play anything and people would give me money," he said. For example, a song that sounded like an Irish ballad but was actually about space aliens. Or one about a man who replaced his own failing heart with an artichoke heart.

Or this folkish ditty, "Cerebellum," about brain damage:

> Oh Cerebellum-bellum
> Don't you leave me behind
> Oh, won't you please be good
> Like you know you should
> And ease my worried mind.

But now that the Old Economy has returned and is not doing so well itself, Mr. Homa is making much less. When he talks about paying the rent now, he makes quote signs with his fingers while saying the words. And he has had to resign himself to crowd pleasers, though not exactly the obvious ones. For example, last Friday, he launched his set with a furious rendition of "Misirlou," from the movie "Pulp Fiction." This led to "I Got You," by James Brown— a tune not often heard on an acoustic guitar—and to "Sing, Sing, Sing," the big band standard.

After half an hour, he looked down at the floor and into his change cup, which doubles as a foot-cymbal to keep the beat. "I think I just made 80 cents," he said, with mock enthusiasm.

Of course, he still has a small coterie of devoted regulars. Ailin Kojima, a shuttle rider and a big fan of Mr. Homa's for two years, walked up on Friday and quietly slipped a crisp $50 bill into his hand. "He cheers me up," explains Ms. Kojima, an account manager at a marketing firm. "He's kind of shy and sweet and he has that small town feel to him."

Yesterday morning, his medley of songs from "Star Wars" got things off to such a good start that it almost felt like the old days again. After he played "Folsom Prison Blues," one man whooped and said, "Johnny Cash, *yeah!*" before dropping a dollar in his pot, and then an attractive blond woman told him admiringly, "I'm amazed you can do that while the train's moving."

But despite a good morning, Mr. Homa says he has decided that it's high time to step off the shuttle for good. He is now looking for a full-time job—nonmusical, please—so that he can pay the bills, chase his musical dreams and ride the subway like normal people do.

Perhaps the words from one of his own songs express his feelings best:

> *My friends and my neighbors they ask me for money*
> *I'm broker than they are, I laugh cause it's funny*
> *Oh who do they think I am, some damned Easter bunny?*
> *I'm only a subway musician.*

—ORIGINALLY PUBLISHED JANUARY 15, 2002

SOUTHBOUND WITH BLOOMBERG

Before this one, it is probably fair to say that all 17 men who served as mayor of the city of New York since the subway opened in 1904 at least pretended to be subway riders, some more convincingly than others.

Mayor George B. McClellan boarded the very first train and took the controls himself, driving under nervous professional supervision all the way from City Hall to Harlem. "Well, that was a little tiresome, don't you know?" he said later, setting the tone for his successors.

Fiorello H. La Guardia used the subway, along with babies and baseball, as a handy political prop but not as a regular means of conveyance.

Edward I. Koch said he took it at least once every two weeks, but people did not believe him, and he had to write letters to newspapers insisting that it was true.

Rudolph W. Giuliani liked to take the subway when feeling nostalgic, riding with his son, Andrew, to Yankees games. But their more frequent means of getting to the stadium was riding in something that seemed almost the size of a subway car, the mayor's massive white Suburban, with a police light flashing on top.

Considering this tenuous relationship between mayors and mass transit, there was a great deal of skepticism when Michael R. Bloomberg pledged last year to take public transportation every day he went to City Hall, if the voters would only send him there.

The widespread assumption was that public transportation, in the mind of a successful billionaire, probably meant a taxicab, in which he would have to forgo the legroom and minibar selection of his limousine.

But in the three weeks since he has been in office, Mr. Bloomberg says, he has taken the subway to work all but one day, with little fanfare or attention, generally only in the company of two large men with curly wires leading into their ears and a couple of hundred other citizens of his city who have crammed themselves into his car on the Lexington line.

Mr. Bloomberg's press secretary swears that it is so, and probably the best indication that it really is true is the way the mayor responds when asked whether he enjoys riding the subway. He looks at the questioner as if he has asked about a minor dental procedure.

" 'Enjoy' isn't quite the right word," he says.

Accompanying Mr. Bloomberg on his way to City Hall one morning last week helped to demonstrate amply why he feels this way. It is a testament to something—maybe principle or civic pride or progressive thinking or just plain old masochism—that he has decided to become the first subway-riding mayor.

The station nearest his town house on East 79th Street in Manhattan is the 77th Street station, which means that, even among subway riders who feel themselves beleaguered by crowding, Mr. Bloomberg has joined the vanguard of the oppressed, the Lexington line riders, whose morning trains are usually the most packed in the city.

Last Thursday morning, the mayor left his house a little after 7 with his beige overcoat buttoned to beneath the knot on his maroon tie, like a well-heeled Cheever character. He stopped off for a cup of coffee and swiped his MetroCard through the turnstile. He usually gets to the station at least an hour earlier, but he had decided that morning to mix some campaigning into his trip, stumping at the station for a fellow Republican, Assemblyman John Ravitz, who is running for State Senate in a coming special election.

The 77th Street station can be chaotic enough on a slow day, so the campaigning showed the mixed blessing of having a mayor as a fellow straphanger. It is possible that your station might be a little cleaner than before, but it is also possible that you will enter the station to have a man yell three times into your ear as you go through the turnstile: "Say hello to the mayor of New York City and Assemblyman John Ravitz!"

At a little after 8, the mayor, his bodyguards and a group of aides and reporters made their way to the platform. A No. 6 train pulled up that appeared far too crowded to enter, but Mr. Bloomberg plunged ahead like a linebacker, positioning himself in a corner near the conductor's cab, where he was less likely to get jostled. (He points out that he is no subway neophyte; during the 15 years when he worked for Salomon Brothers, he took the train every day. "And that was back before air-conditioning," he stresses.)

On the way to Grand Central, where he jammed himself into an even more crowded No. 4 train, Mr. Bloomberg chatted with a seated elderly woman after the surging crowd shoved him up next to her. "God bless you," she said, appearing a little flustered to find herself suddenly knee-to-knee with the chief executive of her city.

The woman sitting next to her was more representative of the true spirit of the subway. Sleeping, she cracked one eye open, appeared annoyed that there was so much talking going on, and promptly fell back to sleep.

Gilbert Cruz, a property manager who was standing next to the mayor, beamed. "Look at him," he said. "He's interacting with the public, no problem."

—ORIGINALLY PUBLISHED JANUARY 22, 2002

AROUND THE WORLD IN 40 HOURS (OR "I CAN'T BELIEVE I'M DOING THIS")

At 6 a.m. yesterday, a 17-year-old Brooklyn high school student named Harry Beck got on the subway.

If you are reading this before noon today, there is a good chance that Harry Beck is still on the subway, probably somewhere beneath Brooklyn or Queens, badly in need of sleep, with a sore back, a weak cell phone battery, a ringing in his ears and a subway map on which most of the lines have been inked over in blue ballpoint pen.

The pen marks mean that Mr. Beck has traversed these lines sometime during the previous 24 hours, and if he is lucky—if he has not been stranded in a stalled train or accosted by gangs of high school bullies or fallen asleep on a bench at Coney Island—he will be close to marking off the last line on the map, and ending a very, very long subway ride.

Most people take the train to get to work. Mr. Beck is taking it, more or less, to get to college.

In truth, there were easier research projects he could have conducted to complete his senior thesis at the Packer Collegiate Institute in Brooklyn Heights, near where he lives. But Mr. Beck loves the subway, its history, its mythology and its minutiae, with the kind of love many teenagers reserve for their headphones and their girlfriends. (He even runs his own subway Web site, and in his bedroom, plugged into the wall, is a real, working subway signal.)

So, he thought, why not attempt the transit Everest—468 stations, 230 route miles, 30 to 40 hours, Van Cortlandt Park to Rockaway Park, with everything in between—and see if someone would give him school credit for it, too.

"I mean, some kids are writing about French cuisine or 'This is me going skiing every weekend at my country house,' " he said yesterday, in Hour 4 of the project. "I like riding the subway. So why can't I do that?"

As a literary exercise, it was not the first subway endurance test. The novelist Paul Theroux once spent a week riding the system from end to end, and imparted his most important survival technique, given to him by a friend: "You have to look as if you're the one with the meat cleaver." (This was in 1982.)

As a research venture, Mr. Beck's trip was not exactly Darwin aboard the Beagle, although he did decide to take pictures and notes and to count the homeless people he came across on his journey (10 by 10 a.m. yesterday, on 11 different trains). Mr. Beck also decided not to try to break the world record for navigating the whole subway in the least number of hours, which now hovers down in the low 20's.

Yesterday at about noon, however, he was thinking that perhaps he should have. He was growing a little fatigued. He had tried to get a good night's sleep the night before the trip, and had even swallowed two allergy pills to knock himself out, but he was far too revved up and finally drifted off at 4 a.m., an hour before he had to get up.

"I can't believe I'm doing this, actually, now that I think about it," he reported at about Hour 6, sitting on a No. 2 train, across from a woman watching him suspiciously as he wrote in his subway notebook. "I mean, what a *weird* thing to do."

Mr. Beck does not look the part of what transit workers call a foamer, meaning someone who loves the subway so much that he appears rabid when discussing it. He has long, black, rock 'n' roll sideburns and was traveling with a Weezer CD in his portable stereo yesterday, packed into his green knapsack along with $27 in cash, two bottles of water, gum, breath mints, nose drops, eyedrops, a radio scanner, gloves, a cell phone, his typed-out itinerary and two books for a class he is taking called "Death and Dying." ("It's pretty much a big downer, that class," he said.)

Of himself, Mr. Beck said, "I'm not king popularity, but I'm not a loner either, like some subway guys. I'm not getting beat up in school or anything because I like subways." His physics teacher, Flo Turkenkopf, confirmed this. She says he knows there are things he loves that make him a geek, "but he has a sense of humor about it all."

The school's administrators and Mr. Beck's parents, a psychologist and a former teacher, had less of a sense of humor about his plans to skip two days of school to do something that usually lands other teenagers in a truancy office.

But they were eventually persuaded after Mr. Beck explained the valuable lessons he would be learning in sociology and urban affairs. Plus, he agreed to schedule in lunch and dinner breaks and have a teacher ride along with him overnight.

Reached last night by cell phone somewhere on the L train, Mr. Beck reported that he was faring well, that he had passed through about 230 stations or almost half and, as a bonus, had seen many good-looking young women on their way home to Williamsburg.

Next, he said, he was headed back to Brooklyn to eat dinner at his house. "You know, for my mom," he said, unconvincingly. "To calm her down."

—ORIGINALLY PUBLISHED FEBRUARY 26, 2002

MASS-TRANSIT MOSES

When people speak of having a bad subway day, it is generally understood that the day in question took place in the subway.

For Anthony Trocchia, this is not the way it works.

In fact, he explains, having trouble in the subway—on a subway train, dare he dream—would be a minor victory, something to be savored while stuck in the tunnel.

It was just after 9 a.m. yesterday, and he was explaining this in a humid corner of the Jamaica Center subway station, laughing the way people sometimes laugh to emphasize how thoroughly unfunny something is.

This was because Mr. Trocchia had found himself, once again, feeling a little like Moses.

Not to conflate subway platforms with the promised land, but if you make your way around New York in a wheelchair, as Mr. Trocchia does, and you would like to do so in the subway—using the 38 stations that transit officials have spent hundreds of thousands of dollars over the last decade to make accessible for disabled riders—reaching the platform is the minimum requirement.

Mr. Trocchia would not be able to do that yesterday morning. He would look down a short staircase and see the platform stretching out in front of him. He would see the E train pulling in. Then he would look at the elevator door in front of him, the one with the ragged red plastic tape stretched in front of it.

And he would slowly turn his motorized wheelchair around for a trip back to the street.

"Welcome to my life," he said, "and all its dysfunction."

In the interest of full disclosure, Mr. Trocchia, 33, who has muscular dystrophy and has been unable to walk since he was 11, is not just any guy in a wheelchair trying to use the subway. He is president of an advocacy group, Disabled in Action of Metropolitan New York, and he had invited a reporter to meet him in Jamaica yesterday to explore the workings, or nonworkings, of the subway from the perspective of a wheelchair seat.

He had not set out hoping to find dysfunction. In fact, Mr. Trocchia—who regularly rides city buses and says they work very well for passengers in wheelchairs—had chosen one of the most accessible stretches in the subway, three stations in a row along the E line in Jamaica.

Before he left his home in Brooklyn, he had called the New York City Transit hotline that provides information about broken elevators and had learned that no problems had been reported at any of the three stations. Indeed, at Jamaica Center around 9, it seemed as if things had improved since the last time he had tried, and failed, to use the subway: The elevator from the street worked when he pushed the button. (Mr. Trocchia rolled into it with the caution born of experience. "You never know what the odor du jour is going to be," he warned.)

But the mezzanine, and the all-too-literal red tape stretched across the entrance, turned out to be a harbinger for the rest of the morning.

Stoically patient, cracking jokes in a musical voice, Mr. Trocchia made his way back to the street and rolled eight blocks down Archer Avenue to the Sutphin Boulevard station, which is listed as being wheelchair accessible on New York City Transit's Web site. And indeed, in theory, one might concede that it is accessible, except that the elevator is in the middle of a construction project and has been shut down for several months.

Mr. Trocchia began buttonholing employees to see if they knew of another elevator, but his questions were met mostly with blank stares. A helpful New York State Police officer offered to get a partner and carry the wheelchair down the stairs, until he was told that it weighed 300 pounds. "Oh," he said, and then added, when asked about the elevator situation, "I have no official comment."

Mr. Trocchia rolled on. ("Thank God for Paxil," he said.)

His last attempt of the day was made at the Jamaica–Van Wyck Station, where the elevator was working but the button at street level was not. Mr. Trocchia waited for the elevator to be brought up from the mezzanine, where the button did work. But upon reaching the platform—at 10:20, more than an hour after he started trying to take the subway—he was finally defeated by the obstacle he had known he would find all along. The thresholds of the arriving trains were about 4 inches higher than the platform, making it almost impossible for Mr. Trocchia to enter the train without his chair flipping over backward. A platform riser, which has been installed in some other accessible stations, was absent at Van Wyck, meaning that the elevator did little more than provide a meaningless sightseeing trip down to the platform.

Mr. Trocchia, smiling a little sarcastically, mentioned that an elevator was scheduled to be installed in the subway station nearest to his home in Williamsburg. "I think it's supposed to be done in 2012," he said, smile widening. "I guess I'll put my plans on hold until then."

—ORIGINALLY PUBLISHED JULY 23, 2002

RESIDENT COMIC

It has been one of the longest-running performances in the history of the subway.

Nearly every morning and evening for the last 12 years, from the depths of winter to the dog days of summer, a very bitter, disturbed and funny man named Carl Robinson has taken the stage at a narrow, overcrowded theater otherwise known as the subway station at Fifth Avenue and 53rd Street.

The morning show begins with the rush. The evening show can last until midnight. Sometimes there is singing, but usually there is just the stentorian voice of Mr. Robinson, booming out a monologue that falls somewhere between scabrous stand-up comedy and postmodern performance art. On good days, it is reminiscent of early George Carlin. On bad days, especially when Mr. Robinson recalls the many women who seem to have wronged him, the material veers toward late Lenny Bruce and commuters tend to veer away from him.

But even those who are not fans of Mr. Robinson (and he has his share of very angry critics) have come to think of him over the years as an institution at their station, as inseparable from it as the subterranean funk or the steep escalators.

So last Monday, when the morning rush arrived and Mr. Robinson was not there to greet it, some people began to wonder.

Tuesday passed without him, then Wednesday, and rumors began to swirl on the platform and in nearby offices that he had been attacked or struck by a train.

"Everyone is thinking he is dead," said Mohemmed Khan, who manages the station's newsstand and stood in it yesterday shaking his head sadly. "Every day, thousand people and thousand people more ask me, 'Where is Carl? What happened to Carl?' "

Sybil Ferere, an administrator at a nearby brokerage firm who has given Mr. Robinson food and money for years (he does not panhandle), said that by midweek she was so worried she called the police. "I just couldn't believe that Carl wouldn't be there to talk to us every day," she explained. "I had to find him."

Ms. Ferere eventually did, in a hospital: Mr. Robinson had been attacked, in the early-morning hours last Monday as he slept on the platform, by a man who tried to rob him and then returned and cut his throat open with a knife.

The good news, however, was that the subway's comedian-in-residence could not be silenced so easily. He was at Bellevue, very much alive and healing well. And, as he demonstrated himself last Friday, sitting up in his hospital bed, his attacker did not manage to sever his sense of humor.

"The doctor told me that they cut off only my head," he reported, smiling weakly, "so luckily no vital organs were touched."

Removing his neck brace to reveal a six-inch horizontal row of stitches across the middle of his throat, Mr. Robinson said that he was certain that he was going to die as he stumbled, bleeding, down the platform to find a pay phone. (The police are still searching for his attacker, whose face Mr. Robinson said he did not see clearly.)

"You know what I was thinking?" he asked. "I was thinking of this girl I know who doesn't like me very much and how I would never get to see her again."

Propping himself up with a pillow, Mr. Robinson explained

that he came to be homeless and living in the subway about 15 years ago, for reasons that he did not care to discuss in detail. He would say only that after a few years as a clerical worker, he came to a powerful realization: "I watched a lot of people go broke, and I thought that I would just stay broke and bypass the process."

He decided to settle permanently at the station at Fifth Avenue and 53rd Street for purely practical reasons. "The acoustics," he explained. "My voice carries very well there." And thus began what Mr. Robinson calls his Fifth Avenue Show, subtitled "Free as long as you pay the $1.50."

He sees himself not merely as a comedian, however, but as a voice crying in the wilderness, revealing the truth behind the day's events and trying to disabuse comfortable New Yorkers of their comfortable illusions. "Most of these people I see," he said, "they're living in cages. The cages are very nice. They're made out of gold. But they're still cages."

As something of a misanthrope, Mr. Robinson is not quite sure what to make of all the attention and concern that many of those delusional and caged people have exhibited toward him since his attack.

Ms. Ferere phoned him. A worker at the newsstand, Mohemmed Youshuf, went to the hospital to visit him last Thursday. And Mr. Khan, the newsstand manager, even put up a sign in the station to let commuters know what had happened to Mr. Robinson.

It says: "Mr. Carl. He is in the hospital. He is okay."

"Carl is a good man," Mr. Khan said. "A very, very funny man."

Whether he will be funny once again on the platforms beneath Fifth Avenue remains uncertain. But Mr. Robinson hinted that if he returns, he will be better than ever.

"The cut on my throat has improved my voice," he said cheerfully. "Can you believe that?"

—ORIGINALLY PUBLISHED AUGUST 20, 2002

TANGOS WITH MANNEQUINS

It is not easy being the hardest-working man in subway show business.

It means starting the day, as Julio Diaz does, in a tiny basement room in Corona, Queens, that is about as wide as a subway car but much shorter. This room is his kitchen, his living room, his bedroom, his workshop and his rehearsal hall.

In it, there is a bed and a television and a window the size of a takeout menu. There are pictures and newspaper clippings ringing the room like wallpaper, showing Mr. Diaz with Tito Puente, Mr. Diaz with Celia Cruz, Mr. Diaz with his adoring crowds. There are albums of thank-you letters and certificates from places like the Smithsonian. And there is a huge box of prized videotapes, several of which Mr. Diaz played yesterday morning to demonstrate his durable renown: glowing interviews with him on Japanese television and Colombian television and Telemundo and CNN.

As he was doing this, however, he was interrupted by the sound of a toilet flushing from the common bathroom down the hall, and one of Mr. Diaz's neighbors, a small man in a red tie, shuffled by, brushing his teeth. "Buenos dias," the man said, through his toothbrush.

"Buenos dias," Mr. Diaz said, sullenly.

And with that, he began stuffing a suggestively dressed mannequin that he calls Lupita into her Samsonite suitcase and limbering himself up for another day on the job.

If there were a way to measure the distance between fame and fortune, the subway would undoubtedly be one of the places where the chasm between the two yawns the widest. Performers there can be seen daily by enough spectators to pack a small stadium. They can bask in the kind of adulation usually reserved for rock stars. Because of the iconic position the New York subway holds not only in the city but also around the world, they can become cult heroes and minor media stars.

But while a few escape to careers aboveground, many more find that subway fame, as great as it may grow, does not translate well to auditoriums where the walls are not tiled. What remains is something that occurs to few subway riders when they pause to watch their favorite performer: a steady working-class job.

The job may be more interesting and rewarding than most, but it is a full-time job nonetheless, as demanding as they come. And if anyone ever decides to draw up a seniority list for such jobs, Julio Cesar "El Charro" Diaz, the ubiquitous subway mannequin dancing man, will surely be at the top.

"It's my only work," Mr. Diaz explained in Spanish yesterday afternoon, before taking the stage for two hours of almost uninterrupted tango, salsa and mambo on the mezzanine at the station at 34th Street and the Avenue of the Americas. "Me and Lupita, we are out there every day, every day. We work very hard."

So hard, in fact, that if you have ridden the subway any time in the last eight years—since Mr. Diaz left the suburbs of Bogotá, Colombia, and decided to seek his fortune in the subway—it has been hard to miss him, his black dress shoes permanently tethered to the high heels of the 30-pound female mannequins he manufactures himself on an ancient Singer sewing machine in his tiny apartment. (As with B. B. King's procession of guitars, all named Lucille, there have been numerous Lupitas over the years. Mr. Diaz said he now keeps six, repairing them as he rapidly wears them out.)

Despite the laughter and applause that follow Mr. Diaz every time he draws his partner from her suitcase, he acknowledges that many subway riders have never quite known what to make of a grown man dancing with a buxom, life-size doll, even if the man dances very well.

"They think that I am lonely or a sad man," he said. "They make jokes about what I do with the doll when I am alone."

But Mr. Diaz points out that his kind of dancing has roots that long predate him or the subway. As a young man in Colombia, he remembered, he and others would dance the "baile de la escoba" or broom dance, a folk tradition in which couples pair up to dance but they are always one woman short. A broom takes the place of the missing woman, and the dancer who ends up with the broom in his arms when the song ends has to buy drinks for everyone else.

The way Mr. Diaz became a professional dancer with inanimate partners sounds like a folk tale itself: a friend of his had lost a beautiful girlfriend to the handsome son of a shoemaker. He asked Mr. Diaz to make an effigy of the woman and dress it in her old clothes, so that he could burn it in the street and rid himself of the painful memory of her.

But before Mr. Diaz's friend could burn the effigy, he decided to take one last, drunken, dance with his lost love. And the crowds watching on the street went crazy with applause.

"That is when I decided once and for all," Mr. Diaz said. "The next doll I am going to make will be not to burn but to dance with."

He shrugged yesterday between dances and wiped the sweat from his face. "And so," he said, "here I am today."

—ORIGINALLY PUBLISHED SEPTEMBER 24, 2002

LEFT OUTSIDE LOOKING IN

If it is true that great art is born of great suffering, what happens when there is only a little suffering?

In fact, what happens when the suffering is so common that tens of thousands of New Yorkers probably experienced it this very morning and the plot of their collective tragedy could be summarized like this: Hero hurries into subway station, hero sees train, hero runs for train and misses train. Doors close abruptly in hero's face with a dirgeful ding-dong. Flourish. Exeunt motorman, conductor and train.

It is clearly not the stuff of Antigone or even Edvard Munch (though screaming with hands clamped to head is a way that many tragic heroes have been known to react to missing the train).

The misfortune is infinitely smaller, more personal and more trivial. Yet when a New York video artist named Neil Goldberg began several years ago to notice the faces of people in the subway as they missed their trains, he was struck by the miniature portraits of loss that he saw on platforms all around him.

The loss, of course, was only that of a ride in a crowded subway car, and another would be along shortly to offer the same inglorious opportunity. But the faces seemed to resonate something more than urban impatience—something about fate itself, about how we all view ours, even as reflected in the most mundane daily transactions.

As Mr. Goldberg describes it—in a way that places a missed subway squarely among the subjects of the world's greatest art—the experience is about nothing less than "what happens when you want something and the world has other plans."

So since this summer, Mr. Goldberg, 39, has been venturing into subway stations with a handheld Sony video camera to record these ubiquitous three-second transit dramas. He has stood by stairways and doorways from 125th Street to Atlantic Avenue in Brooklyn, waiting for the subway to come and for the small, bad thing to happen to his fellow citizens.

"Sometimes," he admitted the other day just after 7 a.m., filming at the West Fourth Street station in Manhattan, "I almost find myself rooting for people to miss the train—and that's not really something you want to be doing with your life."

But over weeks of filming, often during the most sweltering

mornings of the summer, he has learned several things. Among them is that capturing quintessential images of subway disappointment, in a system awash in them, is not always easy. Sometimes, he would film for three hours, with trains arriving every five minutes, and would leave with only one good shot. ("That liberal door-opening policy," he complained jokingly the other day, as a nice conductor held the doors open for latecomers.)

He also found that the reactions of those who missed the train were a lot less operatic than he had expected. People grimace or roll their eyes. They exhale loudly. Some look around, as if for moral support. Sometimes they just look painfully embarrassed and smile strangely, as if they have done something stupid to cause the doors to close on them.

Most interesting and striking in some of the 17 hours of footage Mr. Goldberg has taken so far is the way that commuters briefly let down their subway masks, allow their faces to register real emotion and then, realizing where they are, quickly bring the masks back up again.

"It makes it almost hard for me to watch sometimes," Mr. Goldberg said last week in his studio, where he will eventually distill the hours of recorded faces into probably five minutes of pure disappointment. "Somehow, it's almost sad."

His past work, some of which has been shown at the New York Video Festival and on PBS, has also dealt with these forgotten corners of human emotion, a theme he often classifies under the heading of "Hallelujah Anyway," a title of one of his previous gallery shows.

In essence, he says, it is about how "life can be an insane and depressing drag and thank God for it."

He has, for example, videotaped storeowners in the weary early-morning ritual of hauling up their security gates. He has taken a music box around the city and filmed it in various places playing the hymn "How Great Thou Art." He is at work on a documentary about what he sees as the almost mystical nature of Wall Street futures trading.

Mr. Goldberg said he tried once before to do a project in the subway, in which he wanted to ask token clerks to read a piece of Whitman's "Song of Myself" through their microphones. (It includes a passage that sounds almost as if it is referring to the subway: "Stout as a horse, affectionate, haughty, electrical, I and this mystery here we stand.") In the end, though, the Metropolitan Transportation Authority decided not to allow its clerks to partake in any literary moonlighting.

It is unclear what the agency thinks of Mr. Goldberg's latest project, but most subway riders, when told about it the other morning at West Fourth Street, simply shrugged and kept their subway masks firmly in place.

"Personally, I don't get upset when I miss the train," said Steven Badice, a dealer in women's garments. "There's always another one coming."

—ORIGINALLY PUBLISHED OCTOBER 8, 2002

TAKING THE TRAIN HOME

Paul Kronenberg of Sheepshead Bay, Brooklyn, says he is trying hard to break out of "this subway buff syndrome," the one that has held him in its stubborn grip for at least 50 years now.

But it cannot be easy, especially when he goes to sleep each night and rises each morning to see a motorman's cab from an old subway car bearing down on him from a corner of his bedroom like a rail-bound Flying Dutchman.

Or when he heads to his kitchen, past a subway sign in the hall that says "To the Trains." Or when he looks at his broken player piano, atop which sits a destination marker from a D train, seeming to announce that his piano is Coney Island–bound.

One afternoon last week, he gingerly stepped around his latest creation, a sizable piece of evidence that his subway fascinations have not, in fact, faded at all: a life-size reproduction, on his living room floor, of an elaborate 1904 Times Square mosaic, rendered in construction paper instead of tile. He estimates that he has painstakingly cut out and pasted together more than 2,500 tiny pieces of paper so far.

"Wow," he observes, pausing to consider this fact. "I really *am* crazy."

If so, Mr. Kronenberg is the kind of crazy many New Yorkers long to be. In a city filled with people who live to work, often to their detriment, he has carefully worked only enough to live exactly the kind of life he wants to live. (For the last nine years, he has been a math tutor, "yet another in my line of underachieving careers," he says with sheepish pride.)

This painstaking reduction of ambition has allowed Mr. Kronenberg, in a city teeming with part-time buffs of everything from egg creams to elevators, to become something of a rarity: a full-time buff.

He might not know the names of every kind of subway car to have rumbled beneath the city, as some buffs seem to. He might not be able to describe in excruciating detail, as some can, how the Chrystie Street connection severed the Nassau Street Loop in 1967.

But Mr. Kronenberg, 58, is still believed to be the only man in the five boroughs who has collected the salvaged parts of an old subway car and, adding only lumber and dark-olive paint, built a highly faithful mock-up of a motorman's cab in his own bedroom, complete with controls, windows, a folding gate, an express sign and a hand-operated windshield wiper. You might think of it as the subway version of the Johnny Cash song, "One Piece at a Time," about an auto factory worker who assembles a Cadillac from spare parts.

"When I show it to people," Mr. Kronenberg says of his creation, "right away they know that I'm not married."

He built the cab more than two decades ago, while working as a driver for a Brooklyn company called the Brighton Laundry, which had a plant near the huge Coney Island subway yard.

The process of getting the parts was, he recalls, only slightly more complex than it might be today if they showed up on eBay, though far less legal: "They were selling off all the old cars for scrap and there was this young foreman. Basically, you'd go up to the door and tell him what you wanted and he'd tell you what he wanted, you know; and you'd come to some sort of agreement."

Today, the cab shares Mr. Kronenberg's cluttered blue bedroom along with an old Fairbanks, Morse tube radio, a reproduction of George Tooker's famously creepy painting "The Subway" and shelves full of books on topics ranging from existentialism to "How to Survive Your Parents."

He said the cab has been sitting there so long, at the foot of his single bed, that he notices it no more than he would an old Barcalounger. So he is always a little surprised by visitors' startled reactions to it.

"I tend not to show it to people right away," he admits, "because I'm afraid that it might freak them out."

This solicitude, though, appears to have more to do with courtesy than real fear of what people might think of Mr. Kronenberg, who said he long ago made peace with the fact that he was paddling up a tributary far from the mainstream.

Or as he put it, his eyes twinkling through the thick glasses that make him look a little like the cartoonist R. Crumb: "I have no image problem. I don't take myself seriously enough to have one."

After delving over the years into other odd areas of research—old radios, Greyhound buses, cash registers and Otis elevators—Mr. Kronenberg said last week he had found two new ones that might help supplant his subway obsession.

One is Skee-Ball, the old-fashioned arcade game, a version of which he is considering building intact in his living room. The other, he says, smiling, is a very nice woman from Texas, whom he met recently and who seems to appreciate some of the very things he appreciates.

He is still uncertain, however, whether a motorman's cab, a Skee-Ball alley and a new woman friend are completely compatible in the life of just one Brooklyn man. "Something might have to go."

—ORIGINALLY PUBLISHED NOVEMBER 5, 2002

THE SAW MAN

It was Good Friday, and at the end of the Union Square subway station near the police office, the one-man ministry of Moses E. Josiah, maestro of the musical saw, was getting under way.

He was playing one of his favorite instruments, a 28-inch, two-octave solid steel tenor saw made by the Mussehl & Westphal specialty saw company of East Troy, Wis., whose newspaper advertisements once encouraged musically inclined readers to "amaze your friends with this sensation of radio, vaudeville, orchestra and lodge."

Since its heyday in the 1930's, the saw has mostly disappeared from those forms of musical entertainment. A couple of the forms have disappeared as well. But Mr. Josiah, who taught himself to play his father's handsaw at 17 in a village on the coast of Guyana, has never wavered in his devotion to the haunting powers of a humble household tool.

It might no longer show up much in soaring concert halls, he says, but the saw is perfect for that vast musical venue known as the New York City subway, for several reasons. Among them: it is easy to carry, it is hard to break, it does not have a high resale value and not many people realize that beautiful music can be played on a handsaw, making it a great crowd pleaser.

But the best reason of all is that the sound is wonderfully subway-proof. While guitars, saxophones and even trumpets lose decisively in decibel contests with approaching trains, the notes of the musical saw rise above the roar, something like the chime made by rubbing the rim of a crystal glass.

"People have told me that they can be at the other end of a station and all of the sudden they can hear me, like I'm right next to them," he says. "They say it sounds like the voice of an angel in their ear."

Every day that he plays, but especially on this Friday, that is the analogy Mr. Josiah is hoping his listeners will make. He hopes they will hear a holy message emanating from his saw. In the process, he also hopes that this gratifying message will make them grateful enough to throw a few more dollars into his bag. It has been a very slow winter.

"I can play the calypso, and I can play the classical," he explained, rubbing rosin from a white box onto his worn violin bow. "I can play anything you want. But today is a sacred day, and today is for gospel."

A reporter looking for Mr. Josiah heard him long before seeing him, picking out the sounds of the hymn "He Touched Me." Mr. Josiah, 74, was seated on a small black folding chair, hunched slightly over the saw, which was laid across a white hand towel on his left leg.

The saw handle lay against his right leg, which moved like a violinist's fingers creating vibrato, as his right hand bowed the flat edge of the steel.

The saw, a gift, was once gold-plated, Mr. Josiah said, but the gold has mostly worn away with use. On the top of the blade, these words are engraved: "Maestro Moses Josiah, Master Sawyer."

"I didn't give myself the name maestro," he explained. "All over the United States and the world, that is the name they have given me. I know the Lord blessed me. This is a gift he has given me."

As the afternoon wore on, Mr. Josiah used his gift tirelessly for several hours. He labored over "The Holy City," and "Master, the Tempest Is Raging," particularly appropriate just after noon, when it seemed that trains were pounding into the station, and into his head, every three seconds. By 1:30 p.m, Mr. Josiah was becoming a little disappointed that his gift was not bringing in a few more gifts of the worldly kind.

Junior Bennett, an office administrator, stopped to listen, transfixed, and gave a dollar. Ihor Slabicky, a software developer, fled from an inferior saxophone performance on the L platform and also contributed. But most of the donations were very small change, and at one point a disturbed woman even tried to give him a piece of bread.

"You know, New York is a very interesting place," Mr. Josiah said, stopping to rest his aching left hand. "Some panhandlers—*panhandlers*—make more money in an hour than I do."

He picked up the bow again and this time decided to venture into a few devotional tunes much more on the nonevangelical side, including "You Light Up My Life," and "Danny Boy." At one point, he turned off the tape player he used to accompany him and did a slow, ethereal rendition of "God Bless America."

"I like to call that version saw-cappella," he said, smiling.

But the biggest crowd pleaser was decidedly his version of "Imagine," by John Lennon, whose lyrics he either did not know or chose to ignore the meaning of. The song drew applause, a handful of dollars and the adoration of a woman who swayed to the music and sang. "Yeah," she said.

Before the reporter left that day, Mr. Josiah thanked him but then called out: "As the Bible says, it's more blessed to give than to receive. Now I know you're not going to leave here without giving a little something, are you?"

—ORIGINALLY PUBLISHED APRIL 22, 2003

SUBWAY WHIZ KIDS

At least by the age of 4, and at least in New York City, children have already begun to emulate their parents in one very noticeable way: they, too, have cultivated obsessions.

For most children, these obsessions tend to be the ones of sunny youth, circa 2003, ranging from Harry Potter to pterodactyls, from Spider-Man to highly specialized science kits. ("What are the basic ingredients of soda pop?")

But for a much more single-minded group of single-digit New Yorkers, there is an obsession far weightier and a list of questions vastly more difficult. So difficult, in fact, that most adult residents of this city will consider them only under duress. For example: When does the Z train run and what is its last stop in Manhattan? Will the W train terminate at Whitehall Street next year? How many connections can you make from the Franklin Avenue shuttle? What is the only subway line that does not go into Manhattan?

To answer these questions and many more, let us introduce our three panelists today on "It's a Subway Whiz Kid." In order of age, they are Alexander Puri of the Upper East Side, who will be 5 next month and whose favorite subway line (at least this week) is the B. Next is Aidan Langston of Park Slope, Brooklyn, who turned 6 last month and is bold enough to favor the V train, making him probably its only fan. Finally, there is Jonah Gaynor, 6, who lives in Greenwich Village and is particularly partial to the G. The three have joined us today because they represent a special class of highly intelligent and high-achieving urban children: They are the smallest subway buffs. Still almost short enough to sprint under a turnstile without bumping their heads, they have forgotten more about the subway than most MetroCard-carrying adults have ever known.

In other cities, children with such an aptitude for geography and transportation might be able to identify different types of S.U.V.'s or navigate the megamall. In New York, subway whiz kids are more helpful: they can tell you how to get from Middle Village, Queens, to Cobble Hill, Brooklyn, in only two transfers.

And this knowledge does not come without hard work. It involves hours of late-night reading. "At 3 years old, in the same way some kids take teddy bears to bed, he was taking the subway map to bed and studying it," said Sandeep Puri, Alexander's father, watching his son the other day as he sat in rapt concentration in the middle of an oversize subway map.

Being a bona fide subway whiz kid also involves untiring field work. Alan Gaynor, an architect, and his wife, Sharon Silbiger, a doctor, have taken Jonah to more than 50 stations. They have explored the wonders of the L line and the joys of the routes to Coney Island. They have twice taken the express bus to Staten Island, just to take it back again. "There are some times," his father reports admiringly, "he's forced me to go to Queens and we've never gotten out of the subway."

As his mother explained, "It's not the destination. It's the process."

She quickly added of her husband and herself, who are not untiring, "For us, the destination is part of the process."

Aidan Langston's father, Chris, who works for a health-care foundation, often enjoys playing Watson to his son's Sherlock on such fact-finding trips. But the other day, in the family's house in

Brooklyn, he asked a quite dangerous question: If Aidan could choose any route from school in Chinatown back home to Brooklyn, what would it be?

His son did not hesitate. His ideal trip, he said, would be to take the F from East Broadway to the Forest Hills stop in Queens, then transfer to the V, ride that to Second Avenue on the Lower East Side and then catch the F at that station back home to Park Slope. (Note to non–New Yorkers: This is like going from Dallas to Detroit by way of Honolulu.)

There was a moment of stunned silence in the house, followed by a burst of adult laughter—laughter tinged with the knowledge that someone would undoubtedly be making that long journey someday soon, because he would insist. (Aidan's mother, a New York Times reporter, was once scolded by her son for eating a knish on the subway. The rules, he reminded her, forbid eating.)

Parents of subway buff children—the buffs are overwhelmingly boys—say that they see the transit system as an excellent teaching tool for a city child. After all, the subway involves colors and numbers and letters. It involves rules and geographical facts and hard-to-pronounce words, like Sutphin Boulevard and Mosholu Parkway.

But for the subway whiz kid, there is a much bigger attraction: knowing more than anyone else, particularly the parents. Like little Jedi knights, the buffs tend to get the Force and then quickly humble their elders. This group includes transit reporters for large metropolitan daily newspapers.

One recently made the mistake of asking Aidan Langston when the Z train ran.

"Only rush hours," he replied.

"What about weekends?" the reporter asked.

Aidan looked weary and disappointed, as if he'd explained this a thousand times. "Are there rush hours on weekends? I don't *think* so."

—ORIGINALLY PUBLISHED MAY 27, 2003

CITIZENS OF THE SUBWAY

SHORT STORIES FOR THE LONG RIDE HOME

Ever since the day it opened, and for obvious reasons, the subway has been as much a supermarket as a means of transportation.

Daily, it delivers a group of prospective consumers numbering in the millions. August Belmont, the system's chief financier, sensed the potential and tried to tap into it by plastering the early subway with hundreds of tin-framed advertisements for everything from rye whiskey to washing powder.

Over the years, there have been cigar stands, flower stands, newspaper stands, hot dog stands, weighing machines, chewing gum machines, a record store and an army of hardworking immigrants who wander the trains selling AA batteries, toy cellphones, lighted yo-yos and plastic sticks that make funny sounds when you wiggle them. Once, this reporter spotted a well-used one-piece bathing suit for sale at the Second Avenue stop on the F line.

So it is in the grand tradition that a small, friendly 27-year-old woman named Adrian Brune set up shop about two months ago to sell her wares at Times Square. Her "shop" is a very common one for low-budget subway commerce, consisting of a small cardboard box, behind which she sits with her back against the wall. But what differentiates Ms. Brune from her competitors are her unique handmade products, advertised in a hand-lettered sign on the sides of the box.

"Struggling writer w/ good short stories for sale: $2 each," it says, adding in parentheses, "Master's from Columbia; bad economy."

In other words, Ms. Brune is a rookie in what the writer Terry Southern once called the "quality lit game," but instead of trying to sell her work through publishers, she is going straight to the reading public. This would be a brave decision, if it were one she made herself. In actual fact, she says, it was made for her by the publishers.

57

She was at the point where she had to start selling her possessions or start trying to sell her work, she said last Friday, sitting on the floor of the Grand Central subway station, where she has relocated because the police there seem to have a deeper appreciation for nonfiction prose than those at Times Square. ("I've only been kicked out of here three or four times," she said with appreciation in her voice.)

Ms. Brune, who was raised in Tulsa and came to New York by way of Chicago and Boston, says that she originally conceived of her subway sales job as a form of "protest slash performance art." After graduating from Columbia University's Graduate School of Journalism last year, she tried in vain to find full-time work but landed only occasional freelance jobs. She was angry at New York, she said, and wanted to find a way to let the city know it.

But then a funny thing happened: she discovered that low-priced, cheaply copied, heartfelt short memoirs held together with paper clips actually sell pretty well in the subway.

In fact, on good days she sells out of them, unloading 20 copies or more of each of her three stories. (One is about the death of her stepmother, with whom she was very close; a second is about online dating and a third is about a whirlwind romance she had with another woman at Columbia. She is at work on a fourth story about another romance.)

Last Friday afternoon, Ms. Brune was doing a very brisk business in the corridor leading to the Times Square shuttle. As a salesperson, she tends to comport herself with ease, something like a country-store clerk selling overalls to farmers.

"You like short stories?" she says to the undecided. "Try this one."

"Hey, have a good one now," she says as they walk away.

When a man in a baseball cap walked up, she gave him her friendly sales pitch. "You want action or satire?" she asked.

"Action," he said finally and forked over two bucks for the

whirlwind romance. Ms. Brune folded the bills into her pocket. "Guys like the action story," she said.

In the space of about two hours, she had sold more than a dozen stories, some to satisfied repeat customers like Orlando Fonseca II, who had also bought the whirlwind romance story and gave it a big thumbs up. "It reminded me of some of the stupid things I did," he told Ms. Brune, smiling.

She says that she has never had any customers demand their money back, though one man did return a story, apparently disappointed that she is gay. "I think he was a little sweet on me," she said.

Of course, the subway is not always the most genteel sales environment. Once, she spent the whole afternoon with a rambling drunk at her side. The same day, she said, "a slam poet—or whatever he was—came up and slam-poeted me."

Some people, most often women in business suits, look at her behind her box, well dressed and well fed, and roll their eyes. But others seem to understand. In fact, one woman recently gave her a $10 bill for a single story.

"O.K., maybe she thought this was about charity," Ms. Brune said. "Or maybe she just thought I was undervaluing my work."

—ORIGINALLY PUBLISHED JUNE 10, 2003

SUBWAY SCHOOL

The following are not the kinds of things you typically find at a subway station:

- A poster warning that pinkeye might be going around.
- A nice woman handing out apple juice.

- A group of Brooklynites sitting in a circle, singing, "The more we get together, the happier we will be!"
- A group of Brooklynites weeping openly. (O.K., you might actually find this in the subway.)

But if you go to the Prospect Park station on the Q line in Brooklyn, and choose the wrong door, you may find all of these things just about any weekday morning, along with even more unusual sights.

For example, if you had been there yesterday morning, you could have watched as a Brooklynite named Colin Hamingson stared thoughtfully out a window at a subway train, and then, in a kind of experimental gesture, licked the window.

"I like the subway," he announced.

It is highly unlikely that you will walk through that wrong door at the station. The people behind it have put an electronic lock on it, and a second door behind it with a second lock, because as much as they do not want random people wandering in, they want even less to have anyone inside wandering out and onto the subway.

That is because many of those inside are just learning how to say "subway." Some still wear diapers. None of them have MetroCards.

They are charges of the Maple Street School, a 25-year-old nursery school that moved in September into an old retail space inside the station, making it probably the only subway-station nursery school in the country.

In the process, the school placed two of the biggest worries of many New Yorkers—commuting and child care—in close proximity in a daring effort to ease both. The aboveground subway station is on the other side of a thick wall and so it is not easy, once inside the school, to tell that you are still, technically, in the subway.

There are some reminders, though. In a fire stairway, there is a patch of the original tile work from the station, circa 1905.

Sometimes you can hear the roar of the train, even over the roar of 40 toddlers. As in the subway, there is also a smattering of graffiti, though in the school it is in crayon, not spray paint.

Undoubtedly the best interface with the subway is in the upstairs rear of the school, where a small window allows one to gaze right down onto the open-air subway tracks.

For an urban child of a certain age, this window is better than television and almost as good as chocolate.

"If the littlest kids are crying, it's one of the things we do," said Wendy Cole, the school's director and a teacher. "We put them up there on the table so they can look out. I have one little girl it works like magic for. She's transfixed."

So were Colin Hamingson, 3, and his friends, Cameron Gipson, 3, and Marko Read, 4, yesterday morning. They kneeled side by side at the window, like a panel of experts, closely studying a motionless Franklin Avenue Shuttle train on a storage track. Marko Read, speaking for the group, reported, "It's broke, I think."

The parents who run the Maple Street School as a cooperative had always hoped they could move their school closer to the subway. They never expected it to be quite this close.

Ultimately, they chose the site because it was close to Prospect Park and because the appendage to the station had 2,800 relatively inexpensive square feet in which to relocate their school, which has migrated over the years from Midwood Street to Lincoln Road to Maple Street to Nostrand Avenue, outgrowing each location.

Had the parents known what lay ahead in turning part of an almost century-old subway station into a school, they probably would not have done it, said Kendall Christiansen, board chairman of the school.

The space, abandoned for five years, looked like the subway had run through it instead of near it. "As I like to say, it was well ventilated and hydrated," Mr. Christiansen said. There were traces of toxic solvent, left as a kind of parting gift by a former tenant, a dry cleaner. There was the mighty bureaucracy of the Metropolitan Transportation Authority to negotiate. There were grants to cobble together and locks to install to calm parents worried about their children riding the Q train prematurely.

Four years and $850,000 later, the parents can be forgiven for feeling as if their school will never quite be finished. The other day, Mr. Christiansen was conducting a tour when Sarah Prud'homme, a mother of two, entered. "There's this guy outside," she reported, "some kind of a roofer, who says he wants to get paid."

Despite the renovation blues, the parents seem to be exceedingly proud of their pioneering subway school. The children, for their part, take it all in stride. "Of course I go to school in the subway," Ayla Safran, 4 and three-quarters years old, declared. "That's where people go to school."

—ORIGINALLY PUBLISHED DECEMBER 11, 2001

UNDERGROUND GOVERNMENT:
CIVIL SERVANTS AND
SUBWAY SHERIFFS

The gears of the machine: It takes more than 20,000 workers to keep the subways running. Most of them have great vocal chords.

THE LONELINESS OF THE LONG-DISTANCE MOTORMAN

At work last Friday, Wayne McLamore drove 62 miles. This was not so bad, considering that he used to drive 124 miles. And especially considering that his coworkers can sometimes cover 155, which is like driving from Midtown to the Maryland border.

"Seniority," he said, winking. "Seniority does that for you."

Mr. McLamore is not a traveling salesman. He is not a state trooper. He does not drive a tractor-trailer. In fact, the territory he and his colleagues traverse every day does not even take them beyond the bounds of New York City—simply from Queens to Brooklyn to Manhattan, Manhattan to Brooklyn to Queens.

They are the motormen and motorwomen of the A train. And in the world of subway drivers, they are the long-haul truckers.

From its farthest Queens terminal at Far Rockaway to the other end at 207th Street in northern Manhattan, the A line covers 31 miles, the longest run in the system, according to transit officials. (The runners-up are the F line at 29 miles and the D at 25.8.)

If there is a place in the city that can be said to feel like the country, the A is the train that goes all the way there.

It starts within smelling distance of the Atlantic in the Rockaways. It slices across Jamaica Bay, where gulls drop clams on the tracks to shatter their shells. But then it leaves behind its pastoral trappings and travels beneath the shadows of jets roaring forth from Kennedy International Airport. It deposits pony players at Aqueduct Race Track. It veers north into Ozone Park. And then it dives through the dense heart of Brooklyn, goes under the riverbed and rolls beneath Manhattan from end to end.

Mr. McLamore, a former Floridian with a big gold earring in his left ear and 18 years under his belt on the A train, has other responsibilities now, and no longer has to make two round trips through this vast terrain, the way he used to.

"I've got to tell you," he says, "that will take the fight right out of you."

But to spend a morning in the motorman's cab of an eight-car A train with Mr. McLamore as he makes the one-and-a-half-hour trip from 207th to Far Rockaway is still to feel that you have left the subway and found yourself on a less circumscribed means of transportation. "The one piece of advice I give new operators on this train is this: Go to the bathroom before you start," Mr. McLamore says. "It's a long ride."

Mr. McLamore has three favorite stretches. One is the trip across the bay, where in the spring he will sometimes poke his head out of the cab window to take in the salty air. "But don't put that in the paper," he said.

The other two favorites are both long, unfettered straightaways, conducive to speed. One is the express run between 125th Street and 59th Street. The other is the smile-shaped tube under the East River, where the downhill portion can propel the train above 50 miles per hour.

Lou Brusati, the A line's superintendent, had come along that day for the ride, and as the train barreled through the tunnel, you could see him smile in the darkness of the motorman's cab.

"This is the ride," he said.

"Yes," Mr. McLamore agreed. "This is the ride."

(There was a time, back when the subway system was in very bad shape, when Mr. McLamore would drive trains that did not have enough power to make it up the uphill curve in the river tube with a full load of passengers. "We used to have to stop at Canal Street and dump everybody out," he recalled.)

Mr. McLamore does not really have any least-favorite spots along the line, except that for a while he really loathed the Utica Avenue station in Brooklyn, where a man would position himself at the front of the platform every day and launch a large wad of spit at the train's windshield.

There was no violence done, but suffice it to say that last Friday, there was no man waiting to spit on Mr. McLamore's train.

Asked what was the strangest thing he has seen on the A train in his 18 years, Mr. McLamore paused for a minute at the end of his shift. He conferred with the train's conductor, Mary Tillman.

They both decided that it was the pigeons.

"Pigeons will get on at Far Rock looking for food that the car cleaners didn't get," Mr. McLamore said.

"Then when the doors close, they'll take the train one stop and get back out."

"You think I'm kidding, don't you? I'm not kidding. The pigeons take the train."

—ORIGINALLY PUBLISHED JANUARY 23, 2001

PATROLLING THE HOLE

It is not the most conventional method, but a great way to examine how far the New York City subway has come over the last three decades is to consider the medical records of a man named Brendan J. McGarry.

To his friends and family, Mr. McGarry is Joe. To everyone else, for most of his adult life, he has been Officer McGarry. Next year will be his 30th patrolling the place he likes to call "the hole."

Here, presented chronologically, are a few entries from Officer McGarry's occupational injury chart: dislocated shoulder, torn cartilage in right knee, hairline skull fracture, fractured right hand, broken nose, broken nose, broken nose.

The injuries tend to taper off in seriousness and frequency as the years go by, making them a reliable record of not only how violent and chaotic the subway once was, but also how nice and orderly it has been made by comparison.

To spend an afternoon on the beat with Officer McGarry, 53, in the Times Square station is to understand the true distance between these days and what were probably the subway's worst days. For the rest of us, this progress has been a very good thing. For Officer McGarry, frankly, it has made life a little dull.

"You don't want to say that, really, because people can ride the trains again without being terrified," he said. "And I'm no glutton for punishment, but back then? Your blood was always pumping."

"You walked out of the station," he said, "you got a collar."

But now, even when working undercover in plain clothes, Officer McGarry said he might go a whole day or two without making a collar. And even then, the arrest will usually be a fare beater, a class of criminal that is now central to subway crime-fighting strategy. Back in Officer McGarry's youth, he said, fare beaters generally did not merit more than a dirty look.

"They'd laugh you out of the station," he remembered. "They'd say, 'Get out of here with that. You're not bringing that in here.' We were bringing in rapists, muggers, murderers. Some very bad people."

Officer McGarry came to policing as a young man with a more complex understanding of bad people than some. He was born in Dublin. His family moved to New York when he was 3. By the time he was a teenager, he was a member of a mostly Irish street gang called the Crusaders, an affiliation that helped him make up his mind about what to do as an adult.

In other words, the judicial system made up his mind for him. "The judicial system said to me, 'Son, you need to make up your mind, and if you know what's good for you, your mind will be leaning toward the military.'" (Officer McGarry would not elaborate on his youthful offenses. "No convictions," he stressed. "If I'd been convicted, I wouldn't be in this uniform today.")

The United States Marines took him to Vietnam, and his experiences there opened Joe McGarry's eyes to the once-unthinkable possibility that he might actually make a good police officer. He started in 1972, a year the subways were so violent that his cadet class was pulled out of training early to lend a hand to the overburdened force.

His first arrest, he said, should have been a clear indication of what was to come. It was in the Rector Street station on the Broadway line. A huge, bearded construction worker was on the subway platform, roaring drunk. ("Even sitting down, this guy is taller than I am standing up.") Officer McGarry asked the man to calm down. He asked him to calm down again. The man's response was to poke his index finger through the hole in the "P" on the brass Transit Police insignia on Officer McGarry's uniform.

Over the next several minutes, the man proceeded to smash Officer McGarry into every one of the candy machines that used to sit along the Rector Street platform. To Officer McGarry's credit, he did not let go of his suspect. And before the man could drag Officer McGarry up the steps of the station, a token clerk came out of her booth and beat the man into submission with a metal folding chair.

The dislocated shoulder and wrenched knee were the results of that first arrest. The other result was that Officer McGarry, trying to handcuff the construction worker, ended up getting confused and handcuffing two police officers together, "which I heard about for the next four years," he said.

Just for contrast, here, briefly, was the scene on the beat with Officer McGarry last Thursday beneath Times Square. The radio crackled. He sped to the situation. The problem? The mostly well-heeled crowd trying to jam down onto the N and R platform was much too big.

"Why are you keeping all of us from going down to the platform?" a woman asked Officer McGarry.

He smiled, mischievously.

"We get lonely," he told the woman. "We figured this way we could have a conversation."

—ORIGINALLY PUBLISHED FEBRUARY 27, 2001

WHAT IF YOU ARE THE SICK PASSENGER?

Orin Faison is a very nice guy. He is 33. He lives in the South Bronx. He will talk your ear off if you give him a chance.

But if you are a passenger on the Lexington Avenue subway line, you do not want to make Mr. Faison's acquaintance.

In fact, among the people you do not want to have even a brief relationship with in the subway, Mr. Faison probably ranks somewhere between an arresting police officer and an escaped convict.

This is absolutely no reflection on him. It is because getting to know Mr. Faison generally means just one thing: that you have become "the sick passenger," the one referred to in all those signs that ask the slightly sickening question, "What if You Are the Sick Passenger?"

And if you are anything like the hundreds of other sick passengers whom Mr. Faison has come across and helped in two and a half years working as a rush-hour emergency medical technician in the subway, it means one or more of these things:

- That you have fainted, either because you are pregnant or overheated or undernourished or overweight. Or because you just donated blood. Or because the morning after arrived a little too hard on the heels of the night before.
- That you have fallen—either because you fainted or tripped or were tripped or were in too much of a hurry—and that Mr. Faison has collected four of your missing teeth from the platform. (This happened at the High Street station in Brooklyn, when a woman fainted and fell face first onto the concrete.)
- That you have almost fainted or fallen, but instead you just threw up. (Mr. Faison carries a red plastic bag for those who somehow manage to avoid this special indignity until they get off the train.)

It also might mean something much worse. A few months after starting his job, Mr. Faison rushed to the aid of a man in his early 60's inside a train in the Bronx. The man was lying partly beneath the seats, shaking, apparently in the middle of a seizure. As Mr. Faison examined him, the man lost consciousness, stopped breathing and went into cardiac arrest. Mr. Faison started CPR but the man made it only as far as Lincoln Hospital, where he died.

"That was my very first one," Mr. Faison said solemnly the

other morning at Grand Central, waiting for the next sick passenger to come his way. "It kind of shook me up."

Mr. Faison—a big, compassionate man who sees disfiguring accidents lurking wherever he looks—belongs to a small crew of subway E.M.T.'s who were posted on the platforms beginning about three years ago.

The motive behind hiring them was not exactly Hippocratic, as officials at New York City Transit will fully admit. But the subway is not in the business of providing medical care, they point out. It is in the business of getting passengers from place to place, safely and with some speed. This means that if a passenger falls ill on a train, of course transit officials want to get him into the hands of medical professionals.

But with equal ardor, they want him off the train so it can keep moving all the comparatively healthy passengers. With this goal in mind, the medics are stationed at nine of the most packed stations in Manhattan, Queens and Brooklyn.

John G. Gaul, who oversees the numbered subway lines, said a 15-minute wait for the city's Emergency Medical Service during rush hour at these stations can mean that as many as 13 trains will stack up behind the one stalled with the sick passenger.

The trains could be carrying as many as 2,000 passengers apiece, which means that one sick person could be delaying about 26,000 people behind him. Which increases the chances that a couple of those 26,000 are going to pass out, too, from sheer stress. In other words, sickness breeds more sickness.

"The highest percentage of sickness happens at the busiest stations, during the busiest times, in the peak directions," Mr. Gaul said.

During his time underground, Mr. Faison has become something of a sociologist of sickness. He observes that people tend to fall ill on Monday mornings more than on any other day of the week, probably because of weekend excess. They fall and hurt themselves at night and on Fridays, probably also because of excess of some sort.

Despite New Yorkers' legendary impatience, those riding near a sick passenger tend to show incredible compassion, he said. They offer their bags or roll up their coats for pillows. They use their newspapers as fans. They offer a lot of chocolate and orange juice.

"People think that sugar can always keep someone from going into seizures," Mr. Faison said, adding, " 'E.R.' Way too much 'E.R.' "

Sometimes, he said, forward-thinking people also help the sick passenger by helping themselves a little, too.

"They've picked the guy up, they've got him right near the door when the train gets into the station. And they're like: 'Here you go. This is for you.' And then the train pulls out again."

—ORIGINALLY PUBLISHED MARCH 13, 2001

THE SCIENCE-FICTION TRAIN

You have probably seen it. And like the people on the F train platform last week, you probably stopped and stared and tried to squint through the windows at the people inside it, their faces bathed in a blue computer glow.

It is far too short to be a real subway train. It is far too clean to be a work train, the kind that shuffles through stations in the dead of night, full of soot-covered crewmen.

It purred into the station, at Seventh Avenue in Brooklyn, the other morning, and when its blue-and-silver door opened, one expected science-fiction smoke to pour out and the crew to emerge in space suits.

Instead, from the mystery train stepped a very earnest man named Marcelo Vargas, with a neatly knotted tie and a clipboard.

And when he explained exactly what his train does, it was easy to see why he was placed in charge of it.

"This car measures the geometry of the tracks," he said.

"It is called Track Geometry Car No. 2," he said.

"We have two of these cars," he added.

It is that kind of methodical precision that New York City Transit likes to see in the job that Mr. Vargas does: making dead sure that the rails upon which a few million people a day move through the subway system are straight and smooth and as close to 56 and a half inches apart as two pieces of steel can be after being rolled over endlessly by 70,000-pound cars.

What happens, exactly, when the geometry of the tracks is bad instead of good?

"The train could actually fall down to the ground," Mr. Vargas says helpfully.

"That is called a derailment."

He invited a visitor aboard his train that morning and set off south toward Ditmas Avenue on an easy run, to calibrate some equipment. The single-car train—which cost $2.5 million, weighs 45 tons and has logged more than 50,000 miles in the last decade—had just finished a full rail examination earlier in April, sniffing along every inch of active track in the system, more than 600 miles. It was time to get it back into shape for the next trip.

Onboard, beeping and glowing in the darkness of the tunnel, was the kind of equipment generally associated with jets and space shuttles, not old-fashioned wheels on steel.

A laptop computer produced what looked like electrocardiogram squiggles, the lines charting whether there were bumps in the rails, whether the rails were at the same elevation and whether they were the correct distance apart.

A spinning laser on the front of the car limned the edges of the tunnel, measuring to make sure that the bulging concrete walls didn't come too close to the top of the train. And another device filmed the tunnel ahead with a heat-sensitive camera. On the television screen attached to the camera, workers in the tunnel appeared as bright red specters. Signal lights looked like red supernovas. And occasionally, the man who monitored the heat camera, Noel Rivera, spotted a tiny red flash that betrayed a gap in a rail, where it should have been conducting electricity but was not, throwing off a system that tracks the trains' locations.

"It's the equivalent of unplugging your toaster," Mr. Rivera said. "You ain't gonna get toast."

The car—which sometimes has to wait in the dark through long, silent stretches while passenger trains get out of its way—has almost everything its occupants need. There is a tiny kitchen, with a microwave and a minifridge. There is also a bathroom, but it doesn't work. It is stuffed full of hard hats and stacks of paper. "We don't use it," said Rick Melnick, who drives the train. "Because then we'd have to clean it."

Occasionally, even the highest of the high tech needs a low-tech corrective. The car pulled into the sunlight that morning. Mr. Vargas, Mr. Rivera, Mr. Melnick, a data analyst named Norman Crossdale and three other crew members squeezed out of the train and down onto the tracks with a thing that looked like a giant slide rule. It was a rail gauge, to measure the distance between the rails by hand for comparison with electronic readings. (While on the tracks, Mr. Rivera, a very meticulous man himself, spotted a pile of tiny bones. He bent down. "It was a rooster," he said. "You can tell by the spurs on the leg bones." He paused. "Probably from one of those voodoo rites.")

Back aboard the train, it turned out that the technology was trustworthy. The electronic meters were accurate to within one sixty-fourth of an inch. And so the train headed back to the Seventh Avenue station, where its arrival was once again greeted like the sighting of a U.F.O.

"People do stare," Mr. Crossdale said, then shrugged his shoulders. "At least they can see where all their money's going."

—ORIGINALLY PUBLISHED MAY 1, 2001

THE SHERIFF OF GRAND CENTRAL

He is not a long tall Texan. He is more of a square, substantial one.

And he does not wear a 10-gallon hat, as the song says. But it is almost that serious: a big black felt Stetson, bought at Shepler's Western-wear store in San Antonio, where Glenis Shadrick, 59, was born and raised, and where he says he will spend a lot more time just as soon as he rids himself of this obsession with ensuring that trains—specifically New York City subway trains—run on time.

Lots of people who regularly ride the Lexington line have come across Mr. Shadrick over the last five years, usually standing on a platform in the station at Grand Central Terminal. He wears his big black hat. Below it he wears a string tie, a big gold Transit Authority star on his shirt pocket and a belt buckle the size of a small dinner plate. The people who have seen him have wondered: Does that guy really work for the Transit Authority? Or is he just acting out some elaborate sheriff fantasy in the subway?

"Howdy, marshal," said one woman last Thursday, grinning as he herded her into a No. 4 train.

"Ma'am," Mr. Shadrick said, touching a thumb and finger to the brim of his hat.

As it turns out, Mr. Shadrick comes by his shiny badge as honestly as he comes by his Stetson. (He used to wear boots, too, but they hurt his feet too much.)

For the last 14 years, Mr. Shadrick has worked for New York City Transit, first as a motorman, in uniform, and now, with some seniority under his belt, as a plainclothes train service supervisor, a title that hides a multitude of responsibilities.

For the most part, it means that he is the law on the Lexington line, from Bowling Green all the way up to 125th Street. It means that when he gets on the radio, slung across his chest like a bandoleer, and wants to know where an errant No. 5 train is, someone somewhere finds out fast. And when he stands on the platform at Grand Central and stares down the brim of his hat at a man, commanding, "Get your arm outta that door!" the man takes it out posthaste.

"That wasn't that man's train," Mr. Shadrick explains, sounding as moral as Gary Cooper. "He's got reservations on the next one."

The man eyes him warily. "I think people look at me and they think, 'This guy's got to be somebody,'" Mr. Shadrick says.

Last Thursday afternoon, unfortunately, being somebody, even the sheriff, didn't seem to be enough to bring order to Dodge. A No. 5 train, somewhere down south, had a pair of busted headlights and was being taken out of service. This was stalling all the trains behind it and causing the northbound platform at Grand Central to become dangerously packed. It was 5:30, Mr. Shadrick's high noon.

"It's a bad day," he announced to a cute young rider he had seen before.

"How can you say that?" the woman asked. "You just saw me, so that means it's a good day."

"Well, darlin', you're right," he said charmingly. "But it sure is a bad day for the trains."

Mr. Shadrick never exactly expected to be doing this in the New York City subway. He grew up in southern San Antonio, where the closest thing to public transportation during his youth was a boy giving his friends a lift on a tractor. His father owned a feed mill and a few cattle, and Mr. Shadrick remembers a lot of unloading of hay trucks. ("Lord, did I unload hay trucks.")

At 17, he left school and joined the Coast Guard, which is where he stayed for the next 26 years, moving to places like Gulfport, Miss., and Adak Island, Alaska. At the end of his career he went to Governors Island, at the foot of Manhattan, and discovered, to his surprise, that not only did he like it, but so did his children. So after retiring, he decided, why not stay here and try something new? He had always loved trains, he said, and before he knew it, he was driving one, beneath the streets of New York.

What will Glenis Shadrick do when his work is done here?

He says he plans to retire in three years, buy an S.U.V. and just drive, with his wife. If he retires in the summer, he will drive north; in the winter, south. He will also buy a little place in San Antonio, to spend part of the year. Until then, you can find him in the subway, with his hat on.

"Texans, as a rule, don't assimilate," he explains, adding, "The best thing somebody could do for me when I die is bury me in San Antonio with my boots on."

And the hat? "The hat will live on long after I'm gone."

—ORIGINALLY PUBLISHED JULY 10, 2001

MAN BEHIND GLASS

It is not easy to project human warmth from behind bulletproof glass. Especially when the glass has a big bullet hole in it, right at forehead level, reminding the guy on one side that people on the other side have been known to carry more than money and want more than tokens.

Robert James, the guy behind the glass every weekday morning at the 205th Street D train terminal in the Bronx, explains about the hole: "That happened way before I started working here."

"People wouldn't want to do that to me," he says. "At least I should hope not."

It is probably a safe bet. Yesterday morning about 8 a.m., one of Mr. James's customers bowed her head against the thick glass and offered him a half-second silent prayer before buying her token. "Bless you," she said into the metal speaker.

"Bless you," said Mr. James, who had bowed his head, too.

Another woman blew him a kiss. "Hello, sweetheart," Mr. James said. He whispered: "She just had a baby, she and her husband. After *nine* years, they had another one."

Later, a man showed up and passed a $5 bill through the slot, asking Mr. James to hold the money for his son. The man's son came by an hour later and Mr. James, recognizing him, passed along the cash, playing neighborhood banker in addition to token clerk.

It is one of about half a dozen roles he has played most mornings for the last 19 years, all while locked in an underground, fluorescent-lighted, soundproofed, burglar-alarmed box about the size of a small half bath. It is his office and his mess hall. It is his library and his living room. It is where he got a phone call last year telling him that his father had died.

It is also among the most uninviting setups for sociability anywhere in New York City. But, somehow, Mr. James has managed to turn it into a town hall. He has become one of those rare people whom big, anonymous cities sometimes produce: a civil servant so friendly, so ever-present, so clearly enjoying his job that he becomes almost famous for it. (Vacationing in the Bahamas once, he was spotted on the beach by a man who started yelling, "Hey, Mr. Token Booth Man! Mr. Token Booth Man! I know you!")

As such, Mr. James, 47, has become a kind of symbol in the

fight that the Transport Workers Union has been waging against New York City Transit, which has announced plans to reduce staffing and hours at 122 subway token booths citywide, including the permanent closing of 35, to save money.

Can a MetroCard vending machine and a full-body turnstile make sure your teenage daughter gets on the train safely, the union asks? Can they call the police to report a man passed out cold in the bathroom, as Mr. James did yesterday?

Can they serve as confidant and confessor, as part-time police officer, as the Virgil who guides lost pilgrims through the Inferno of the new subway map? ("No, baby, the B doesn't go there no more.")

In other words, can the machine beat John Henry?

The answer, of course, is that it cannot. But unfortunately, there are also not many other token clerks out there who can pull off a John Henry quite as exuberantly as Mr. James, a thin, talkative man who wears blue alligator-skin boots and subway-map ties. There are not many clerks, for example, who, at their own expense, decorate their token booths in theme décor every month.

Yesterday it was American flags and fake roses with fake dewdrops for Independence Day. For Kwanzaa, it was kente cloth. For August, the only month for which Mr. James cannot locate a holiday, he does the booth up anyway, in what he calls "summer-fest" colors, green and yellow.

"You must have an atmosphere that makes you feel congenial in what you're doing," he says.

And occasionally, the decorations even come in handy, as when he had the booth decked out for Father's Day with fatherly gift things: belts, ties, pipes, combs. Along came a young subway rider whom Mr. James knew, on his way to a job interview. "But I looked at him and his hair was nappy and his pants were hanging off his rear end and he didn't have a tie," he recalled.

"So I gave him a tie and a belt from the booth and I told him to get in the bathroom and comb his hair.

"I said to him, 'Listen, you've got to go down there and sell yourself.' And you know what? That man got that job."

Because Mr. James cannot devote such personal attention to everyone, especially when the rush-hour lines begin to lengthen, he likes to inscribe inspirational verses, most of his own invention, on the message board behind him. Yesterday's were some thoughts on the power of the artist. ("A true artist uses more than one kind of canvas. He is not afraid to experiment or try something new.")

At the bottom, he had added, "Today is Masterful Monday."

"What's tomorrow going to be?" he was asked.

"I'm not sure yet. It could be Tenacious Tuesday or Take-Time-to-Know-Yourself Tuesday."

"But I know one thing for sure," he said. "It's going to be a fabulous Friday."

—ORIGINALLY PUBLISHED JULY 31, 2001

TUBE WALKERS

It has always been strange, walking back and forth across the bottom of the East River in the middle of the night.

"Sometimes," Frank Ortiz says, "you can hear the tugboats, going by above you."

The 53rd Street river tunnel, which runs between Manhattan and Queens, seems like something Dante imagined for the Inferno, the place where every sin has a corresponding punishment.

But looking down the river tunnel, it is hard to figure out what the sin might be. It is dark. There are things to slip on, like decomposing rats. Every 10 or 15 minutes, a train thunders through, leaving little room to get out of its way. When the train is gone, there is still the third rail, biding its 600 volts.

And if something really bad happens, the only way out is to run to one end of the tunnel or the other. This means that safety is more than half a mile away, in either direction, if you are in the middle.

"Basically," said Mr. Ortiz, who has thought about this, "you kiss yourself good-bye."

He has been a subway track inspector for more than 10 years. His job began to get stranger after the World Trade Center bombing in 1993, when the police realized that an attack in a river tunnel could spread destruction far beyond the subway: It would probably flood a lot of Manhattan, not to mention Brooklyn or Queens.

So in addition to looking for cracks in rails and concrete, which are dangerous enough, Mr. Ortiz and his coworkers were deputized to look for even more dangerous things, like boxes and bags and people who are not supposed to be hanging out at the bottom of the East River.

Now, after the September 11 attack, the tunnel inspectors feel as if the place where they work has become as strategically important as a nuclear missile silo. To get into the river tubes, past the police officers now posted at both ends of all of them, the inspectors must show not only work identification but a driver's license. A log is also kept by transit officials, so that the police know exactly how many people are in the tubes at all times, and who they are.

Mr. Ortiz and his buddies find this a little funny. "There's nobody in the innards of the subway except us," said Chris Fee, a track worker. "Not the cops. Not the firemen. Nobody. We don't even want to be down there."

But behind the veneer of humor, even the toughest track workers worry more now about finding something or someone down there with them. River tunnels, buried beneath mud and water, do not seem to be the kind of shining towers of American might that would attract terrorists. But considered another way, they are just horizontal towers. And if they collapsed, it could cripple the city much more effectively than falling skyscrapers have.

Mr. Ortiz and coworkers were talking about this just before dawn the other morning, as the overnight shift ended and they sat in their locker room at Columbus Circle, changing out of their tunnel clothes, thickly powdered with steel dust.

It is the kind of locker room you might expect for guys who work all night in such a lonely place. There is a centerfold of Shannen Doherty, partially clad, on a locker door. There is a faded sign on the wall that reads, "I'm only laughing 'cause you're my boss." Mr. Ortiz—whose full first name is Francisco, but who is often called Fidel because of his love for Toro Bravo cigars—explained the nomenclature of the track worker.

Tunnels are not the things that run between regular stations. Those long empty spaces are simply called "the hole." Tunnels are the things that run under the river, except that these are more often called tubes. In other words, there are no tunnels.

But whatever they are called and as desolate as they may be, Mr. Ortiz and the others are proud that they are their domain. "Those guys are the eyes and ears down there," said John Samuelsen, the transit union official who represents them. The workers remembered the time in the mid-1990's when the police were after a suspected rapist in Brooklyn and the man dashed into "the hole." The track workers led the chase into the darkness, with the police following.

"This is one of the only places in the city where cops and firefighters can't go on their own," John Tercovich, a track welder, said. "They don't know where they're going. And we're the only ones who know where people could hide."

This is because the track workers have come across all manner of humanity in the subway over the years. Like the homeless man who liked to sit at a Y in the tracks, in a lawn chair, with a battery-powered light, reading The Wall Street Journal. Or the big one who was sometimes seen wearing white Nike sneakers, a baseball cap and nothing else.

Coming across this man in the middle of the night could make the terrors of terrorism seem relative, the workers said.

"It's kind of hard down there," Paul Mondiello, a track worker, said, "to equate what's more dangerous than what else."

—ORIGINALLY PUBLISHED NOVEMBER 20, 2001

THE WATER GUYS

There are all kinds of bad things to worry about in a subway system that never closes. Collisions, derailments, track fires, power failures, crime waves, the size of the rat population and the size of the rats in that population, just to name a few. But there is one danger that riders never seem to consider as they crowd together daily on their way to work: the danger of drowning.

This is not because it is impossible or even outlandish. Look at a subway map and consider how Canal Street got its name. Notice the proximity of many subway lines to huge bodies of water. Understand that most tunnels lie below the water table. Then go dig a moderately deep hole in any of the five boroughs and watch how quickly water seeps in.

The reason few riders ever think about this while in that moderately deep hole called the subway, and why subway seats do not double as flotation devices, is that a small group of underground specialists with rubber hip waders and strong stomachs worry about it for everyone else.

Officially, their department is known as hydraulics, a subdivision of the electromechanical division, which is a subdivision of the maintenance-of-way division. Informally, they are known as the water guys, and as the sign on the grille of one of their trucks will tell you, they like to think of themselves as the "Hydro SWAT Team."

"It never stops," says Joe Joyce, who leads the team. He adds, smiling a crooked George S. Patton smile, "And neither do we."

Their enemy is formidable, unpredictable, destructive and does not smell good at all. Mostly, it is relentless: every day, 13 million gallons of water, enough to fill a medium-size oil tanker, finds its way into the subway. The water guys refer to this, rather casually, as "normal inflow."

Much of it pours in through sanctioned channels, pipes and ditches and sometimes right between the rails, into 280 pump rooms that dot the system, regurgitating runoff, rain and subterranean rivers out of the subway and into the sewers.

Lots of other water, however, invades covertly, bubbling up through cracks in the floor or seeping down from the ceilings, creating stalactites of gunk that look like fourth-grade science projects.

"Nobody wants to see those stalactite things," Mr. Joyce said the other day, grimacing.

But he added, with almost religious resignation, "Sometimes, there's nothing you can do. You never get rid of the water. You just move it around."

If it were not moved around for just a few days, he said, if all of the pumps and special pump trains and trucks were all shut down at the same time to be serviced, most of the subway would shut down in short order, too. "It would not take long," he said, "for it to look like an aquarium down there."

It is a good measure of the kinds of water disasters Mr. Joyce and his crew of 180 workers have faced that after the attack of September 11, when millions of gallons of water poured into the tunnels and nearby buildings, it was only one of the worst floods they had ever seen.

The other day, Mr. Joyce and a maintenance supervisor, John

Swist, returned to the 1 and 9 line beneath the World Trade Center site to check on the progress of drying out the collapsed tunnels. About 95 gallons of water a minute still pours onto the tunnel floor, and is pumped back out through a thick yellow hose that snakes four blocks from Vesey to Murray Street.

"Don't fall in there, because ain't nobody going to come in and get you out," Mr. Joyce yelled at Mr. Swist, who had crouched to inspect a waterfall that was pooling into a gray, brackish, ugly lake in the tunnel.

Both men agreed that if September 11 was the worst they had seen, a very close runner-up in their careers was the break of a 30-inch-wide water main that occurred December 3, 1989, near 135th Street and St. Nicholas Avenue in Harlem, flooding tunnels all the way down to 98th Street and submerging stations up to their turnstiles.

"They had to get a guy in scuba gear to go down in there to shut the thing off," Mr. Swist remembered.

While the water guys love to talk about their glorious battles, they acknowledge that the war against water is mostly one of attrition, of doing things other people would not want to do. Like working with the rats. "Guy not too long ago, a rat jumped on his back and he got so freaked out he fell over backwards and hurt himself, bad," Mr. Joyce said. "He's out on disability now."

The day-to-day job is about clearing potato chip bags from the drain covers and digging soda bottles out of pipes, to make sure that water can reach the sumps where the pumps are. And about once a year, it is about putting on rubber boots, climbing down beneath the tracks and "mucking" all the collected silt from the sumps to make sure the pumps can work.

"What does it smell like down there?" Mr. Joyce said. "Let's just say it's a smell you do not forget."

—ORIGINALLY PUBLISHED NOVEMBER 20, 2001

THE SHUTTLE LADY

The London Underground features a soft, elegant recorded voice that reminds passengers stepping into trains to "mind the gap."

The New York subway features a woman named Millie Mendez who minds the gap for you—whether you want her to or not. That is her job. And her voice is neither recorded, soft nor elegant.

"The gap! The gap!" she cries, the sound carrying like a car alarm. "Be careful or you're going to fall in!"

Ms. Mendez is a platform conductor in charge of one the busiest places in the subway, the Times Square–Grand Central shuttle, on the Times Square end. But there are many platform conductors in many busy places, and so her job description does little to convey what she really does.

Every weekday, 100,000 people ride the shuttle. From about 7 a.m. to 2 p.m., Ms. Mendez's shift, she sees probably 30,000 of those riders, scrambling past her to squeeze into the cars. And while they are within her ambit, almost all 30,000 of them scramble and squeeze in a slightly more civilized manner because Millie Mendez demands it.

She does not carry a gun, a nightstick or a ticket book. In fact, she has very little real power other than the authority to hold trains, summon the police or induce shame.

What Ms. Mendez does have, however, is a voice.

In timbre and volume, it most closely approximates a portable air horn of the type heard at baseball games.

In authority, it ranks with the homeroom teacher no one ever crossed.

In style—her pronunciation of shuttle is a grand, elongated "SHHUUUAAAAAATTLE!"—it is solidly in the urban tradition of newsboys, ringside announcers and people who yell out of high windows.

Ms. Mendez takes no offense at such descriptions. "I was born with this," she says, pointing at her throat. "They tell me I'm the Ethel Merman of the subways."

Before accepting this role, she had worked in the subways for 13 years, starting as a cleaning worker and working her way up to train driver. But on a very bad day several years ago at the Astor Place station on the No. 6 line, she became closely acquainted with the two numbers no one driving a train ever wants to hear: 12-9, radio code for a man under a train, in this case a homeless man who leaped in front of her train just as she pulled into the station.

She never managed to return to driving. "It was just too hard to think about," she explained.

When she got the temporary assignment at Times Square two years ago, it seemed like any other. But then something happened: Unlike other lines, shuttle trains are short, as are the platforms. Its riders are mostly regulars. And because of this, Ms. Mendez quickly found herself on a kind of stage, the kind she did not know she had been waiting for all of her life.

She began to sing out. She began to work the crowd. She began to work up a regular routine, with lines like "Your chariot awaits you!" and "Good morning! Please, don't all talk at once!" delivered to platoons of sullen, sleepy-eyed riders streaming past.

When people do not move into the middle of the trains to her satisfaction, she boards the car herself to show them how. "I'm getting in," she warns. "And I am not a size 10. I am a 24-plus-plus." When someone blocks a door, she says, in a sinister tone, "Please, step away from the door," as if the person had just dropped a pistol.

She does these things every day, regardless of whether there is a reporter following her around. Even when there is, she seems relatively unconcerned. After being introduced to this one, she called him Keith one day and Kenny the next. "Well," she said. "It's close, right?"

Later, she offered him a breath mint. "You need it, honey," she said.

Herman Angel, Ms. Mendez's supervisor, said that when her schedule shifted several months ago and she was transferred to another station, her fans began to complain and letters started arriving at New York City Transit's headquarters, demanding her return.

"She's got, I think, 18 letters of commendation from people in her file," Mr. Angel said. "I've been here 11 years. I think I've got maybe one letter. You know how much trouble it is to write a letter?"

In short order, he said, Ms. Mendez was back at the shuttle, where she is likely to remain as long as her voice holds out.

"A few people," he added, "they don't like her because they say she's too loud. They're like, 'Does she have to talk so loud all the time?'" But those people are probably like the man last Friday morning who crowded near the door of a shuttle train, cutting right in front of 15 people who had dutifully lined up at Ms. Mendez's request.

"Sir," she sang out. "There is a line here."

The man looked murderous but he shuffled to the back of the line while everyone else smiled.

"Men," said Ms. Mendez, shaking her head in disgust. "They just don't like to be told."

—ORIGINALLY PUBLISHED APRIL 23, 2002

WATCHING YOUR BACK

In case you do not have enough things to worry about right now— the subway shutting down next week, your fare going up next spring—Sgt. Randy Stoever would like to give you several more.

First, worry about standing in line near MetroCard machines.

Worry about going through the turnstiles. About getting into a crowded train. About wearing a backpack. About carrying a purse that opens with a side flap. Actually, at this time of year, about carrying a purse at all. Or a wallet or, God forbid, credit cards.

"I don't let my wife carry credit cards," the sergeant said early yesterday morning, in the subway, looking very worried. "Too risky."

In fact, he worries when a waiter at a restaurant takes his credit card away from the table to process it. "Not a good idea," he said. "You should watch him."

Just after 6 a.m. yesterday at the Columbus Circle subway station, Sergeant Stoever met a group of men who looked almost as worried as he did. They shared almost no distinguishing characteristics except that several had mustaches, many chewed gum aggressively and all seemed to dislike ordinal numbers. (14th Street and Sixth Avenue becomes "one-four and six"; 116th and Eighth sounds like a telephone number.)

To an amateur, none of these men looked much like what they were: some of the most experienced undercover antipickpocket police officers in the country, preparing to melt into the subway to help ensure that your purses, wallets and credit cards remain yours throughout this holiday season.

One officer wore a pinstriped vest and a nice blue tie. Another wore stereo headphones, through which the crackle of a police radio could be heard if you stood close. Another wore greasy hair, a goatee and an El Vez T-shirt.

"That's my hippie—I let him dress that way," Sergeant Stoever explained, and then pointed at the man, shaking his head: "You really can't put a suit on that."

The sergeant, who has led the pickpocket unit for nine years, was less expressive—a mock turtleneck, black corduroys and wrap-around shades, giving him the look of a bouncer at a better nightclub. His men, who would rather not see their names in the newspaper, have also been dressed at various times as busboys, bankers and FedEx deliverymen. One plans to dress up soon as an old woman. And if you see a particularly bedraggled homeless man on a train late at night, in a wheelchair, with an eye patch, check for the outline of a 9-millimeter handgun under the dirty blankets.

"Down here," Sergeant Stoever explained, "it's a game of who sees who first."

As the sergeant and his partner began threading rapidly through the morning rush crowds yesterday, ricocheting from 86th Street to Fulton Street and everywhere in between, they were hoping to see several old acquaintances before being seen.

Many of these have been arrested so many times that their unflattering pictures hang on the walls in the subway police station house at Columbus Circle. "Check out this guy," said the sergeant, pointing to a man with a strange facial deformity, a clear drawback in his profession. "Looks like the guy's nose is taking a right-hand turn."

Some pickpockets are known as cutters, old-school thieves who love the thrill of razoring women's wallets from their pocketbooks, leaving them clutching their bags, completely unaware of the robbery. Others are creepers, who do not like to work crowds or jostle their victims but instead follow them out of the subway and are so talented they can steal a wallet, take a credit card from it and then replace it without the victim knowing.

"Some of these people have been picking pockets since they were 12," Sergeant Stoever said. "They know us. We know them. And they all know each other."

Yesterday it seemed as if they had all called one another and agreed to take the morning off, though it was unclear whether to consider this a positive sign or one of an impending blitz.

In their absence, the sergeant and his partner seemed to move at an even more frantic pace, looking for the less evident signs of a pocket about to be picked—signs like subway riders who suspiciously "loop," leaving one car rapidly to enter the next before the doors close.

At Grand Central, the officers spotted a known looper, a red-haired man in an Aztec-print coat whom they had seen some months before. But the man never made a move for a pocketbook. "I think he might just be looking at the girls," the sergeant said. "Sometimes you get those."

They followed other loopers, again with no results. At one point, a reporter was positive that he had seen clear evidence of looping himself. But by the end of the shift, the only pickpocket unmasked was Sergeant Stoever himself, who admitted lifting the wallets of his very own men.

"I've stolen from every one of them," he said, "just to keep them sharp. So they know they can be beat."

The reporter instinctively reached into his back pocket. The wallet was still there.

—ORIGINALLY PUBLISHED DECEMBER 10, 2002

"DROP AND GIVE ME 20"

Somewhere in the coat pocket or the employee locker or the sock drawer of nearly every New York City subway conductor is a 26-page booklet called "Customer Communications and Platform Observation Procedures," otherwise known in subway circles as the blue book.

It is the bible and the Bartlett's Quotations of the conductor. Among the quotations is a classic, on page 6, "Stand clear of the closing doors, please." And another, more obscure but more dramatic, on page 18: "Ladies and gentlemen, this is the conductor. We are delayed because there is a person on the tracks."

Transit officials do not intend these quotes to be edifying but to be memorized and repeated, ideally word for word, any time a conductor presses the intercom button and addresses his or her considerable audience, up to 2,000 passengers on a crowded morning train. The booklet is probably the most detailed on the subject of what should be said when one or two of these 2,000 people decides—out of malice, impatience or stupidity—to hold open the doors of trains.

Conductors can choose, for example, "Ladies and gentlemen, please do not hold the train doors open." Or perhaps the slightly more direct, "Please release the doors so that the train can leave the station." But whatever phrase is chosen, the blue book counsels, "The last thing we want is for a conductor to overreact, and to make an announcement in a confrontational tone of voice."

With this in mind, there was clearly an unscripted moment in progress yesterday morning at the Atlantic Avenue station in Brooklyn, where unseen hands or feet somewhere along the crowded platform were holding the doors of a Manhattan-bound No. 2 train.

A woman's scratchy, angry voice rang through the cars. "Move into the train!" she commanded. A few seconds later this was followed by "You need to MOVE into the train!" Then, erupting like a cheap machine gun, "MOVE IN, MOVE IN, MOVE IN, MOVE IN, MOVE IN!" And then later, with the train still sitting, a more slow and threatening command, like Dirty Harry with a door button: "Let GO. Of the DOORS. In the REAR! LET 'EM GO!" (The doors were finally released. A woman on the platform remarked, admiringly, as the train sped away, "You go, girl.")

This is a subway phenomenon that has existed, of course, ever since trains have been crowded, meaning, essentially, since the first minute the subway opened. But in the last several years, as the number of riders has increased greatly, it seems much more prevalent: the conductor as drill sergeant.

While they do not demand push-ups, these conductors, like drill sergeants, use a wide range of aggressive behavior modification tactics. There is yelling and repetition. There are insults and threats. ("I will call the police!")

There is, perhaps most effective and widely used, shame and demonization. ("You, with the blue backpack, if you just let go of the doors, then all of these nice, tired people can go home.")

Sometimes, however, it simply seems as if the conductor is just taking it all a little too personally. Such as the one Clayton Parker, 15, heard on a No. 1 train announce, "I have no problem taking this train out of service and leaving you suckers on the platform, so let's try again."

Or the one that Laura Napolitano, 19, came across on a Q train the other day, maniacally shouting "Slam!" as he opened and closed the doors rapidly.

Veteran subway conductors explain it is very easy to get frustrated on the job, but some get a lot more frustrated than others. "Some of the people I work with don't—let's see how to put this— don't have all the social graces you might hope for," said Jimmy Willis, a 15-year veteran who explained that he decided many years ago that closing subway doors was just not something he was going to get angry about anymore. And he has seen plenty to make him angry.

He has been spat upon at least 15 times on the job. He has seen high school students ram batteries and pens into the subway door tracks to jam them. He has watched a woman put her baby into the path of the closing doors to make him open them again. Once, he narrowly missed being clocked with a baseball bat. And another time, an impatient passenger actually managed to connect.

"There was an old lady on the platform," Mr. Willis said, "the quintessential old lady, and she bops me on the head with her umbrella. I thought, 'This is it. I've seen it all now.' "

Deborah Hardwick has seen even more in her nearly 20 years in the conductor's cab. She admits she has sometimes played drill sergeant. But now, older and wiser, she uses a new tactic—call it urban bonding—that works better. Perhaps one day it, too, will be enshrined in the blue book. It goes like this:

"It's the end of my day. I want to go home. Just like you do. So if wouldn't mind . . ."

"Thank you."

—ORIGINALLY PUBLISHED MARCH 4, 2003

THE BIG SUCK

Very early yesterday morning while you were sleeping, a group of generally large men got up, got dressed and did some vacuuming for you.

Being generally large, they did not use a small vacuum cleaner: it was 225 feet long, weighed several tons, cost $15 million, sat atop four Detroit Diesel engines and was capable of moving 55 miles per hour. When cranked up, it did not sound much like a Hoover. It sounded more like the end of the world.

Despite the fact that this vacuum had no special hose attachments, it was quite effective in getting at those hard-to-reach places, like the subway tunnel between Jay Street and High Street on the A line.

In fact, over the last two years, since it arrived from France—that nation of progressive vacuumers—this particular vacuum cleaner and an identical counterpart have reached almost every unclean spot in the underground portion of the subway and have a lot to show for it, none of which you would want to be in the same borough with.

Together, they have sucked up almost five million pounds of the gunk and junk deposited daily in the system by subway riders and by the trains themselves, whose wheels leave behind a fine, black steel dust that coats everything—from the garbage to rats to track workers—with what looks like dark-chocolate frosting.

It is difficult to tell whether the following analogy makes them Mets fans or demonstrates a special hatred of the team, but the men who operate the subway vacuum trains like to calculate that all the trash they have suctioned out of the system since they began in 1997 would cover the infield at Shea Stadium to a depth of 27 feet.

Most of the more sizable, interesting and frightening things left on the tracks—umbrellas, cell phones, tennis shoes, hypodermic needles and folding chairs, for example—are usually picked up by advance track crews who walk out ahead of the train with garbage bags and flashlights. But sometimes, as when your home vacuum cleaner accidentally inhales a sock, the vacuum train also stumbles across something bigger.

"You wouldn't believe what we've had," said John J. Doherty, a superintendent. "We've had a wedding dress. We've had mattresses. We've had things I couldn't even identify."

Mattresses? He quickly clarified: "Not a queen-sized. Oh, no, it couldn't do a queen-sized. I'm talking more like a—what do you call it?—a single bed."

After the five-car train thundered into the High Street station yesterday morning just after midnight, Michael Sullivan, another superintendent, opened a door on the side of one bright yellow car to show where these larger incidental items were trapped so that they would not clog the train's filters.

He invited a reporter to put his head into the opening and look around. There were no wedding dresses or mattresses inside. Instead, it appeared as if a small delicatessen had imploded. "You want to take a sample of that home for breakfast?" Mr. Sullivan asked, smiling wickedly.

Basically the only items the train will not pick up, he said, are AA batteries and wet newspapers, because they are very dense for their size. Although the train sucks 70,000 cubic feet of air per minute, creating a violent foot-high dust storm below it, it is designed to leave small, heavy objects behind so that it will not extract the small ballast rocks from the track beds.

Rats, he said, have become very adept at not being extracted, scurrying out of the way just ahead of the lethal suction. "If Ben don't run fast enough, then that's his problem," he said, referring to the long-tailed star of the 1972 horror film "Ben," which seems to be a favorite among the members of the vacuum train team.

About 1:15, after unsticking a stubborn suction hood, everyone climbed aboard and the vacuuming of the subway began, in a methodical two-mile-per-hour crawl south toward Jay Street. The train then reversed and headed north, slowly sucking its way under the width of the East River, a particularly ticklish spot in the system because trash fires could trap riders in the under-river tube, far from any station.

While there are all kinds of special cars that ply the rails of the subway in the dead of night—pump cars, crane cars, tank cars, wash cars, observation cars, de-icer cars, ballast-tamper cars and cars that apply a strange, toothpastelike goo to the rails to keep trains' wheels from slipping—the vacuum cars probably draw the most attention in subway stations. In part, this is because riders find it almost impossible to discern the purpose of the gargantuan yellow train, and because the noise that attends a cleaner, safer subway is truly brain rattling.

Very early yesterday morning at High Street, one homeless man, sprawled on a bench, somehow managed to sleep through the din. Two other men sat with their hands over their ears, looking oppressed.

A fourth removed his shirt, pulled out a rag and began to wash himself, seeming to get into the cleaning spirit.

"When we first pulled in," said Richard Cardiello, a subway

general superintendent, "he was doing push-ups and sit-ups. He's in pretty good shape for a man of his size."

—ORIGINALLY PUBLISHED APRIL 29, 2003

LOST IN THE SUBWAY

Losing something in your own living room is bad enough. Losing something in the street is much worse—the frantic review of the route, the desperate search of the dirty sidewalk, the hope that people are more honest than you have always assumed them to be.

But undoubtedly the worst place to lose something in New York City is the place where you cannot go to get it even if you find it, even if it is just beyond your reach: the track bed of the subway, where neither station agent nor police officer nor firefighter will descend, where the rat holds dominion, where the third rail silently harbors its 600 volts and where a 350-ton train could be right around the corner.

And yet even in that murky and dangerous ditch, there is the possibility of redemption.

In fact, more than three quarters of things dropped down there are found—including, once, unbelievably, the wedding band of a thoroughly drunken man who let it slip from his ring finger between cars somewhere in Brooklyn and was afraid to go back home to his wife without it.

Usually the lost valuables are not so valuable. But if someone still wants something back after it has been on the tracks, New York City Transit will go get it. If it tumbles down anywhere between Coney Island and 23rd Street in Manhattan, the call usually makes its way to a phone in a locked corridor of the DeKalb Avenue station in downtown Brooklyn, where a man with a thick mustache named Mario Trischitta usually answers it.

Mr. Trischitta, 42, has almost 20 years of experience working down where the only people allowed are those who have been trained for five weeks in how to deal safely with live subway tracks. His coworkers, Reggie Corbett and Larry Cummings, have 43 more years of track experience, collectively. They are, as Mr. Cummings puts it, the seasoned veterans, "the firemen of the track division," and the name of their unit reflects it. They are known as the subway's Emergency Response Team.

Arranged in 10 small crews throughout the city, the teams are paid to sit and wait for the worst, and when it happens they are usually the first on the scene for every kind of it: track fires, broken rails, water main breaks and the call they all dread.

"A man under is the worst," Mr. Corbett, 43, said the other day at DeKalb. "Nobody wants to go to a man under."

But in the midst of emergencies and helping to prevent them, the men are also charged with doing the equivalent of what fire-fighters do when they rescue cats from trees. It might not be a real emergency, but it seems so to the cat owner.

In the same way, when a pair of dentures is lost on the subway tracks, it certainly seems like an emergency to the man who uses them to eat.

"People drop their dentures," Mr. Corbett said, shaking his head. "I just don't know how they fall out of their mouths."

People also tend to lose wallets, cash, canes, hats, gloves, books, cell phones, MetroCards, receipts, utility bills and tiny teardrop-shaped earrings. ("Earrings are the hardest," said Mr. Cummings, 48. "Like looking for a needle in a haystack.") Mr. Trischitta usu-ally doesn't ask questions when he retrieves personal possessions, but once he went to get a man's shoe from the tracks. He found the man standing near the token booth, with one socked foot held up gingerly off the dirty floor.

"I had to ask him, 'Guy, how'd you lose your one shoe?' He told me that he was walking and an old lady stepped on the back of his shoe and he took another step and it flew down into the subway." (A lawyer who lives in Brooklyn once lost one of her favorite shoes—a robin's egg–blue Miu Miu mule—in the gap between the train and platform. It was fished from the track bed but before she could retrieve it, a transit employee with no appreciation for high-end footwear threw it away. "I really, really loved it more than I have ever loved another shoe," the lawyer said later.)

The lost-property men are very diligent with their high-powered flashlights, and they find most things they are summoned to find. They once searched all the way from 45th Street to the 59th Street stations on the N line in Brooklyn for a single hoop earring and returned it to a very grateful owner. Sometimes, when they can't find something, they suspect that it has probably been left in another pair of pants, but they keep looking anyway.

Other times, they are asked to find things that they begin to suspect do not belong to the person asking for them.

"You get someone who looks down and spots some jewelry or money or a cell phone down there, and goes and tells the token clerk it's his," Mr. Trischitta said. "You've got to be suspicious."

Then again, the men are also called to collect items that they cannot believe anyone would actually want back, like the 99-cent baby's sippy cup all the way up at 125th Street in Harlem or the beach ball out near Coney Island. "When we got there, it was just a ratty piece of rubber," Mr. Cummings recalled. "But we gave it back to the customer anyway."

Last Thursday was completely uneventful, with no emergencies and nothing lost. On Friday, they retrieved two cell phones and a paperback book. Yesterday, there were four emergency calls, all turning up nothing.

What do they do, sitting in their locker room, while they wait for the calls to come? The men smiled at each other. "We all spend the time wisely, reading through our safety manuals," Mr. Trischitta said. "Of course."

—ORIGINALLY PUBLISHED MARCH 19, 2002

THE LOVE SONG OF NOME J. POEM

Some day it might live again, but for now the Nome J. Poem Subway Art Gallery and Comedy Club has been closed.

Mr. Poem, 53, has been a booth clerk at the High Street station in Brooklyn Heights for about three years, working the midnight-to-8 shift. During his time there, he has become a Magic-Marker Michelangelo, decorating the white greaseboard in his booth with funny drawings and occasional goofy doggerel, usually related to the subway.

> I pledge allegiance to the MetroCard
> And the free rides for which it stands
> Unlimited, underground
> With round trips and transfers for all.

Many early morning riders looked forward to these overnight creations. They had become a brief but reliable antidote to subway stupor. But one morning last week, instead of artwork, riders found a stark announcement on the board, in plain black marker.

It said, "No Artwork."

Anne Samachson, a vice president of a Wall Street brokerage firm, talked to a clerk, and her fears were confirmed: a station supervisor had ordered an end to personal messages of any sort on the greaseboards, which are supposed to be used only for impersonal messages, like service announcements. Saddened, Ms. Samachson called this column to report what she felt was an outbreak of over-active bureaucracy.

"It really brought a little bit of heart and soul down there," she said of the drawings and verse. "It made walking into that disgusting subway station just a little better every day. It's a shame to see it go away."

Reached by phone at home in Brooklyn last week, the curator, administrator and sole artist of the High Street subway gallery said that his creations were simply his way of making the midnight hours pass a little more quickly.

"Basically," he said, "from about 3 to 6, it's just me and the turnstile jumpers and the homeless and the cops."

Mr. Poem—it is his honest-to-God real name, legally changed in 1975 to better reflect his creative nature—enjoys working the graveyard shift, because it frees up his days. But he says that he does need things to occupy his mind until morning.

Sometimes, he brings in a white Fender Stratocaster with a maple neck. When it gets quiet, long after midnight, he plugs it into a battery-powered amplifier and plays until morning.

His god is Jimi Hendrix, whose picture hangs on a calendar in the booth. But more often than Hendrix, Mr. Poem plays the blues. What better music is there, he asks, when you are sitting alone in the middle of the night underneath Brooklyn? (It is not the first time he has played in the subway; in the late 1980's, before he was hired as a clerk, he dressed up in face paint, called himself the Blues Clown and played on station platforms. He eventually quit, he says, because the acoustics were lousy, the money was disappointing and the summer heat melted the spirit gum on his rubber nose.)

Mr. Poem said that he had never been ordered to stop drawing before. And he was always careful to stick to light material that would not offend anyone. "No politics, no sex and no religion," he said. "You can really get people going with those three."

Instead, he would write boosterish slogans about the beauty of the High Street station or protransit messages. When the subway token was discontinued in the spring, Mr. Poem drew an elaborate coffin with a token inside and wrote "R.I.P." below, with the dates of the token's brief life, 1953 to 2003. Another night, he drew a picture of the earth with a crude representation of North America and a line pointing to the Northeast, along with the words "You are here."

"Sometimes, I was on a roll," he said, "and sometimes I was not, you know. I tried to make people smile."

But one station supervisor was not smiling. Two weeks ago, the supervisor—whose name Mr. Poem would rather not mention—ordered the clerks at High Street to remove all personal items from the booth and to stop posting personal messages on the boards, he said.

"I had a set of 10 Magic Markers, all colors, and she told me that I could only keep the black one," he said, adding that she told another clerk to remove the origami boxes he had fashioned out of used MetroCards.

"It was all very letter of the law," Mr. Poem said wearily.

He explained that, under the regulations, clerks are also forbidden to listen to the radio, dim the booth lights or leave their shirttails untucked. So he stressed that he did not want to make any waves about the no-art order. He has been around New York City Transit long enough—14 years now—to know that clerks generally outlast supervisors and that if he just waits quietly for a year or two, he can probably pick up where he left off.

Besides, he said, the supervisor did allow him to keep a small vase for a fresh-cut flower. And, so far, she said nothing at all about his Hendrix picture.

"If that had been removed," Mr. Poem said, "then we would have had a problem."

—ORIGINALLY PUBLISHED JULY 8, 2003

The mass-transit menagerie: In addition to monkeys, turkeys, chickens, dogs, cats and snakes, pigeons sometimes take the train, too.

PIGEONS RIDE FOR FREE

In the annals of strange subway stories—some urban legend, some alarmingly real—there has always been a menagerie of animals.

Stories of alligators roaming the tunnels, of pet snakes loose on trains, of rats strong enough to survive the third rail. There have been eyewitness accounts of live chickens, on their way from poultry market to soup pot, escaping from sacks and running through the cars. A beagle was once spotted transferring from express to local at Times Square, and a monkey was captured in the subway in 1960.

But one subway animal story has been so persistent and widespread that it simply cried out to be investigated: the case of the train-riding pigeons of Far Rockaway.

A little more than a year ago, a motorman and a conductor on the A line, which terminates at the Far Rockaway station, swore to this reporter that it was true. They said it was common knowledge among longtime riders and those who worked on the line. Pigeons, they said, would board the trains at the outdoor terminal and step off casually at the next station down the line, Beach 25th Street, as if they were heading south but were too lazy, too fat or maybe too smart to fly.

The inquiry into this claim began the other afternoon, when the question was put to a car-cleaning supervisor at the terminal. He appeared suspiciously nervous about the subject.

"Oh, no," he said. "Our trains have no pigeons."

But Andrew Rizzo, 44, a cleaner sweeping in a nearby train, looked around and smiled as if he were finally going to get to reveal his secret. The birds ride the trains all the time, he explained, motivated not by sloth but by simple hunger and ignorance: when the trains lay over at the terminal to be cleaned, for about 20 minutes, pigeons amble through the doors, looking for forgotten crumbs. Being pigeons, they do not understand the announcement that the train is leaving, and the doors close on them. They ride generally for one stop, leaving in a hurry as soon as the doors open again.

"If you don't know what's going on," said Mr. Rizzo, pushing his glasses up on his nose, "you'd think they knew what they were doing. It's a little freaky."

Mr. Rizzo has a soft spot in his heart for pigeons, who helped him make a living in Central Park in the late 1980's when he was less gainfully employed. He would strap tiny cups of bird feed to his arms and head and would soon be covered with pigeons, Hitchcock-style. He would put out a donation box, and pull in $200 on a good weekend. "I still feed them sometimes," he said. "I feel bad for the little guys." But he also admitted, "I run them out of the train. I don't want them to make no mistakes, if you know what I mean." Despite his efforts, they make many little mistakes, all over the floor.

Mr. Rizzo and many of his fellow employees at the terminal have become something of amateur ornithologists. They said that pigeons—known vulgarly as air rats, more accurately as rock doves—ride trains at several outdoor terminals and stations, like the Stillwell Avenue station in Coney Island.

Francisco Peña, a conductor on the A, said he has watched them step off his train and promptly fly all the way back to the Far Rockaway terminal. Perhaps not quite as impressive as the blue homing pigeon reported to have flown 7,200 miles from France back to Vietnam in the 1930's. But still not bad, in Mr. Peña's opinion.

Frank Maynor, another car cleaner, noted how the sparrows and seagulls, also plentiful at the terminal, are never bold enough to venture into the cars. The sparrows can be seen hopping onto the threshold, looking longingly inside. The gulls loiter outside, like thugs, waiting to tear pizza crusts from the bills of unsuspecting pigeons as soon as they carry them out.

"They shove the pigeons around," said Mr. Maynor, disapprovingly. "But they're going to evolve and start going into the trains, too. They're giving up a lot of food to the pigeons."

On the subject of evolution, Sarah Canty, another cleaner, said she had noticed that the pigeons might be evolving themselves, into more alert straphangers. "When the bell goes off, you watch them," she said. "They know the bell like we do." And indeed, when the next bell rang, signaling that a train was about to depart, several pigeons could be seen high-stepping it out of the trains.

But there are still pigeons that have either not learned or are yearning to break free from the nest. And at 10:45 yesterday morning, it finally happened: a dark, plump bird with iridescent purple feathers around its neck took a ride.

Alone with the bird in the car was Eduard Karlov, a retired procurement officer for the United Nations.

Mr. Karlov, originally from Moscow, glanced over at his fellow passenger and smiled. "He does not bother me, and, in fact, I find him rather amusing," he said, adding, to his interviewer, "I cannot give you any more details with respect to pigeons, however."

—ORIGINALLY PUBLISHED MARCH 5, 2002

9 LIVES BY THE 3RD RAIL

The search for the Fulton Street subway cat started the other day with a hopeful heart and a healthy dose of skepticism.

For years, there have been clear signs at the station pointing to the existence of a full-time feline resident there—the suspicious absence of mice, for one, but more tellingly the tiny cans of cat food that seem to materialize behind a steel column on the downtown platform of the J and M lines.

A morning token clerk swore that the cat was real and so did a Brooklyn psychologist (my wife), who reported having seen it on her way home from work. But the consensus among conductors was that the cat was just a figment of the imaginations of weary subway riders, particularly of the mysterious woman who left the train around dawn every weekday and carefully set out cans of food for it.

"I think she might be . . . you know?" said one conductor, making the swirly finger sign at his temple. Another conductor said, "I've seen food there for years. I've never seen no cat."

A third said, "I kind of worry that maybe that woman is feeding a rat and she just thinks it's a cat. You never know around here."

With that pleasant thought in mind, a visit was paid to the station and the investigation was formally launched. In short order, it revealed the aforesaid cat food at the edge of the platform—a can of Nine Lives Salmon Supreme Entrée, another of generic-brand chicken and rice, and some dried food, accompanied by a dish of water. It also revealed evidence of a kind of consumption that had cat, not rat, written all over it: the salmon was missing but the generic chicken and the dry food were untouched, apparently disdained.

Carmen Figueroa and her boyfriend, Agosto Astorga, sitting on a bench nearby, continued to be dubious. "I never heard of a cat living in a subway station," Mr. Astorga said. But just then, at around 11:15 a.m. he looked over the shoulder of his questioner and his eyes grew wide. "Oh, dude," he said.

"Oh my God!" Ms. Figueroa exclaimed, pointing. "Look."

Up and down the platform, heads turned. And behind the column where the food sat, another head also turned, a small one belonging to a distinguished, slender gray cat with dark gray stripes and a neatly washed white face, poised gracefully over the salmon. It stared intently at all the people staring in its direction, quickly took another bite and then hopped down onto the tracks, where it perched languorously atop a running rail and began to lick its paws.

It might not have been as momentous as tracking down Bigfoot or the Loch Ness monster, but for some of the station's regulars it was a memorable event nonetheless: the Fulton Street cat had been found.

A makeshift committee gathered near it on the platform and began to debate why it was there.

"Maybe there's a litter of little kittens under there somewhere," Mr. Astorga surmised.

Israel Nieves sized up the cat and concluded otherwise: "He is a hunter. He likes to stay here for the hunt."

Later, Joey Calvanico, a glazier from Brooklyn, seemed to confirm this theory. "He's got a mouse!" he yelled, kneeling on the platform to give the play-by-play. "He's got it under his paw!"

Efrain Ortiz, for his part, wished that those skills could be exported to the side of the station where the No. 4 train stops. "A rat ran right into our train once," he said, grimacing. "We need a cat like this over there."

In the end, no one could quite figure out why a cat would choose to live under the platform of a working subway station and spend its days lounging on the tracks, where it must rouse itself every 10 minutes or so to leap out of the way of speeding trains.

"The only two things I know," said Lawrence Jackson Jr., a station cleaner, "is that somehow or another, he knows not to go anywhere near the third rail. And he's clean. He never does his business up here on the platform."

"Other than that, who knows about that crazy cat?" he added. "He's a loner."

The only person who might have known more was the mysterious woman with the cat food, and with the help of a diligent photographer, she was finally spotted the other morning spreading out the canned sustenance for the day.

But even Muriel Sterbenz of Ridgewood, Queens, the primary benefactor of the Fulton Street cat for the last five years, said she could provide few answers about it, other than a fairly good idea of the sex—female—and a name, which she has bestowed herself: Schatzie, from the German word Schatz, or sweetheart.

"I can't figure out why Schatzie wants to stay in that subway station either," conceded Ms. Sterbenz, a soft-spoken office worker for the State Insurance Department. "But I know one thing," she added. "She sure wants to stay there. People have been trying to catch her for years. She's too fast for the subway, and she's too fast for them, too."

—ORIGINALLY PUBLISHED AUGUST 27, 2002

BLIND MULES

On this date a century ago, New York City was still a metropolis without a subway. But considerable evidence suggested that one was very, very near, and that it was trying hard to devour the city it was designed to help. For example:

Mansions on Park Avenue between 38th and 39th Streets were sinking into the earth, and their facades threatened to collapse. According to an account in The New York Times, inspectors tried to assure residents that the situation posed no real danger, unless, of course, they "should chance to be standing in front of their homes at the time."

Property was not the only thing being swallowed. So were people and animals, at an alarming rate. In the fall of 1902, one Charles F. Allaire, Civil War veteran, accidentally rode his bicycle into an open subway tunnel at Amsterdam Avenue and 65th Street, breaking his right leg. Edward Morris drove a whole car in, at Broadway and 43rd Street. And several months later a runaway black gelding paid the ultimate price to the machine age: he galloped into the subway in Harlem, broke his forelegs and was put down with a police officer's pistol.

With the centennial of the subway approaching—the first passengers boarded on Oct. 27, 1904—it seemed a good time to begin a close reading of the news leading up to that momentous day. And if events from a century ago show anything clearly, it is that our urban forebears suffered greatly for the sake of the mass transit we have inherited. In fact, if the movie "Gangs of New York" tells how the city was born in the street, stories of the subway's construction tell how the modern city was really born beneath them, with great, strange and sometimes deadly labor pains.

They tell about lakes of quicksand in Chinatown and "rotten rock" under Park Avenue. They tell about the unearthing of cedar water pipes and old cannons and ancient skulls, one, according to The Times, with "two full rows of teeth that looked as though they never knew an ache." They tell about a procession of lawsuits and accidents and angry strikes so great they would doom most major projects today.

But the stories also tell of great sacrifice. How, for example, in an era before dump trucks and bulldozers, much of the muscle work was done by pack mules lowered into tunnels in 1900 when digging began and not brought out again until it was finished—many of them going blind in the interim. An article in the winter of 1903 described one such valiant mule, sometimes called Jim by the workers.

"For the last year," the article said, "Jim has never opened his eyes, not even when a blast of dynamite was exploded in his vicinity. And although he must be as blind as a bat to all intents, his drivers say he never makes a misstep."

Some of the tunnel workers did not fare so well: one hallucinated a fire-breathing dog; another quit because he thought he saw a tiger in the tunnels. The articles tell of some very bad luck, too, personified mostly in Maj. Ira A. Shaler, who earned the nickname the "hoodoo contractor" after a dynamite accident and later a tunnel collapse on his watch in 1902 killed five people, wrecked the Murray Hill Hotel and began to sink several art-filled Park Avenue mansions.

That same year, during a tunnel inspection with the chief subway engineer, the major stepped a few inches in the wrong direction and was crushed by a falling boulder.

Most of the misfortunes of subway building were much more mundane. For example, workers had to wade through sewers and contend with man-size icicles dangling from boulders. They had to untangle such a mess of iron and clay beneath 23rd Street that one engineer surmised that more money had been spent on utility pipes there "than under any other thoroughfare in New York, or in the United States for that matter."

Of course, none of the stories go so far as to suggest that New Yorkers, being New Yorkers even then, took ruined streets and gas leaks and collapses and noise and fires and rat infestations with anything nearly approaching good grace.

It was a city that, while part Dodge City—murderous gangs still roamed Kips Bay, commandeering businesses and attacking police officers—was trying very hard to calm down and clean up.

The offices of The Times were flooded with angry subway complaints for years, mounting as the work dragged on. One 1902 article, summarizing, said the public was finally "beginning to ask if, in their case, patience does not cease to be a virtue."

In March of 1903, a gang of ax-bearing men under the command of a police captain destroyed part of a noisy stone-crushing machine near Bryant Park. One night, guests at the Waldorf-Astoria decided they had had enough, too. Awakened by "such a clatter and racket that it was impossible to sleep or have any peace of mind," they complained angrily to the manager, who complained angrily to the Board of Health, which decided to order the suspension of the work.

Somehow, the subway was finished anyway. But even its workers stopped trying to bet on when. "Anyone who tries to say exactly when this work will be finished," one mining foreman said, "is a blamed fool. There's no telling."

—ORIGINALLY PUBLISHED FEBRUARY 25, 2003

BAG OF RATS

There are many different ways to categorize the subway's 468 stations: the oldest, the busiest, the deepest, the darkest, the hottest, the most fragrant.

The other day a group of extraordinarily knowledgeable subway buffs were debating a more subjective and much less desirable distinction: the ugliest.

High on their list was the Wilson Avenue station on the L line, which offers a lovely view of a cemetery through razor wire. Also in contention were 205th Street in the Bronx, where much of the concrete looks like old goat cheese, and the Bowery station, a fittingly corroded shrine to dereliction.

But eventually they came to settle on the Chambers Street station beneath the Municipal Building as the clear winner in their 2003 subway-station ugly contest. Among the online comments from the judges was that the station was "pretty nasty!!!" Another, exhibiting more emotion than attention to grammar, wrote: "OH GOD, it disgusting and it fulls of YUCKS."

A third wrote that there was a good reason the station was used as a setting for the 1984 horror film "C.H.U.D." about a collection of man-eating monsters who lived beneath New York. (In the movie, the letters seemed to stand for "cannibalistic humanoid underground dwellers"; Chambers Street was not, unfortunately, featured in the 1989 sequel, "C.H.U.D. II: Bud the Chud.")

The buffs who awarded the Chambers Street station its dubious crown are in a good position to know. Congregating virtually around nycsubway.org, a Web site, they have photographed and documented the subway over the last few years with more zeal than scientists studying endangered species. They can talk with equal authority about everything from motormen's radio codes to the Malbone Street wreck of 1918 (97 killed in Brooklyn). Their site even offers a translation of a French guide to subway signals, the rare and highly revered "Les signaux du New York City Subway."

But this column still wanted to see for itself whether the station deserved the distinction, and so a recent morning was spent in critical appraisal. The first realization that strikes the visitor upon entering the Chambers Street station is how comfortably roomy it is. The second realization is why: It is almost as big as an airplane hangar and, for most of the day, almost completely deserted. One subway buff, Peter Farrell, compares it aptly to "a bombed-out European cathedral" after World War II.

When it was being built before World War I, Chambers Street was envisioned as a City Hall terminal, a kind of downtown Grand Central at a time when the business and population center of the city was still closer to the southern end of the island. Three years after it opened, its four wide platforms were so overcrowded that one newspaper article described them as "more dangerous during the rush hours than at the Grand Central or the Fourteenth Street Stations."

But by the mid-1920's, the subway itself was pushing the city's population north and leaving Chambers Street far behind. In fact, the station's ridership had dropped off so steeply that half of it was closed by the 1930's.

Walking around the station now, it seems as if half of the station has not been cleaned or repaired since the 1930's, either. Platforms are piled deep with the detritus of the years—an old push broom, a broken umbrella, a toaster and several foothills of soda bottles, all of which could be precisely dated according to the depth of the dark-brown steel dust coating them. In one part of the platform, an original Heins and LaFarge terra cotta plaque of the Brooklyn Bridge seems to have been crowbarred off the wall. In another, the yellowish-white water damage is so extensive it appears that a pack of C.H.U.D.'s has tried to eat its way to daylight.

One regular user of the station, George Moore, an accountant, pointed with disgust to a place where he said he had seen a pile of feces on the platform the day before. He seemed almost dejected that the evidence was missing. "Well, I guess somebody cleaned it up," he said.

But another rider, Jacqueline Chapman, said she had never seen a cleaner at work in the station. "Just the rats picking up stuff," she said, smiling sadly.

This quickly turned out to be no exaggeration—and, in the end, the most convincing argument that Chambers Street is without a doubt the ugliest station.

At the south end of the uptown platform a field of rotting debris stretched for several feet, studded with several full plastic trash bags. As a reporter and photographer watched, one of the black trash bags began to undulate wildly and, over the course of several minutes, as many as a half-dozen rats scurried away from a hole in the top, disappearing into the tunnel darkness.

A bleary-eyed man standing nearby shrugged, and then leaned over the platform to make friendly, squeaky sounds to the rats below. "Just rats," he said.

"You raise the fare to $10, you can't get rid of rats."

—ORIGINALLY PUBLISHED MAY 13, 2003

THE FISH TRAIN

Officially, of course, it will always be the B train.

But just take it on any given Sunday evening, along about half of its southerly course, and you might agree that it would not be much of an exaggeration to give this subway line a subtitle: the Fish Train.

Ramon Vasquez, a hotel maintenance worker, was aboard the train one Sunday. "Whoa, man," he said, making a face. "It smells like fish in here."

Mr. Vasquez was on his way home to Brooklyn when a bracing aroma boarded the B train at the Grand Street station in Chinatown. It got on along with about 20 Chinese-American Brooklynites, each carrying two armfuls of diaphanous, bright orange plastic bags bulging with all manner of food—sweet-potato leaves, flowering chives, slender purple eggplant, brown litchi—but, first and foremost, with fish.

Jin Hua Chung, a 60-year-old steam-press operator, was among the fish buyers. He moved to Bensonhurst from Chinatown five years ago, but he still buys his fish only on Mott Street. "Why?" he said. "Because I like fresh, that's why, and only Chinatown gives me fresh." As he spoke, a good-size tilapia, which had been yanked live from a fish market tank only a couple of minutes before, poked its head from one of one of his orange plastic bags. (He and his wife share kitchen duties, he says but adds, "I am the better cook.")

The Sunday subway fish migration has been growing for a long time now, as Chinese immigrants have fanned out in greater numbers from Manhattan to Brooklyn neighborhoods and yet seem to return en masse to Manhattan on weekends to do all their shopping for the week's meals.

The migration can be seen to some degree on a number of trains that serve other Chinatowns—the N and R to Brooklyn; the 6 train from Canal Street to Grand Central, where the fish make their transfer to the 7 and back to Flushing. But the phenomenon is at its most concentrated, and pungent, aboard the B train, which provides the fastest way to get from Chinatown to Sunset Park, the largest Chinese-American enclave in Brooklyn.

On a nice, late-spring Sunday, it can seem as if thousands of pounds of fish are making their way to Brooklyn along the B, bag by plastic bag, tucked beneath the feet of thousands of riders, bound for thousands of steamers and soup pots.

Among the exporters on Sunday was a 35-year-old man named Wu, waiting by the turnstiles for his wife, who does all the fish shopping for their family. (He is in charge of vegetables.) There was Ying Hsu, a law student, and her boyfriend, Dan Goldschmidt, a lawyer, who had found what they needed and were bound for

Brooklyn. "I just got salmon," reported Ms. Hsu, almost sheepishly. "A very generic American fish."

There was Lisa Mui, an unemployed bartender from Sheepshead Bay who had accompanied her mother on a grocery run. "I love the scene," said Ms. Mui, who had elaborate fingernails and a pierced tongue. "I do love the scene. But to be honest, it's really all about the food." (Later, asked whether the chicken they bought in Chinatown tasted better than supermarket chicken, she rolled her eyes and glanced at her mother, and said, "As long as it doesn't talk to me when I eat it, it's fine by me.")

The contest for most popular whole fish that Sunday seemed to be a dead heat between striped bass and tilapia, a type of African lake fish that is now widely farmed around the world and has become a staple in many Chinese homes. (Tilapia is said to have been the fish that Jesus multiplied along with the loaves to feed the multitudes.)

The contest for most popular shade of plastic shopping bag was not even close: deep jack-o'-lantern orange, which has become a kind of calling card of Chinatown groceries and fishmongers. Bright red ran a distant second and pink third.

Why orange? "Orange is a lucky color," said Kenny Tran, a manager at the Tan My My Market, on the corner of Chrystie Street and Grand, close enough to the subway entrance to hit with a scallop. "Black looks horrible," he said. "And white? You know why people don't use white? Because white is always for the dead."

While Sunday's fish migration seemed festive enough—one man was seen lugging home a case of Budweiser along with his catch—there was a lot of noticeable mourning going on, too, because by the end of the summer, the Fish Train will be no more, at least for a while.

Repairs to the Manhattan Bridge will mean that the B will not run to Grand Street, and the station will be nearly shut down for more than two years. The fish will still make their way to Brooklyn, of course, but probably in smaller schools, on different trains. It might even be difficult to smell which ones.

Mr. Chung, for one, is not happy. "They say this is a developed country?" he said. "If they knew this bridge was going to have so many problems, why couldn't they have built another one?"

—ORIGINALLY PUBLISHED JUNE 19, 2001

4

CUSTOMS, COURTING RITUALS, CEREMONIES, AND HIGH CULTURE

Life in the subway: People have been born there. People have died there. Sometimes, people fall in love there.

READING BETWEEN THE RAILS

There are those who spend their days and nights on the subway because it is more pleasant and less dangerous than where they live, others because it *is* where they live. And there are also those who ride it because it comes with a captive audience, making it a highly effective place to sing songs, sell batteries and save souls.

But New Yorkers also use the subway for another purpose that goes woefully underappreciated: as a reading room. It is certainly nothing new. It has been going on since long before Arthur Miller eased his commute by reading "The Brothers Karamazov"—that "great book of wonder" as he called it—and decided that he was born to be a writer.

But there is some evidence, all of it thoroughly anecdotal, that the subway's use as rolling urban library has expanded over the last several years, in direct proportion to the health of the economy. The theory goes something like this: The good economy makes people happy, but it also makes them work longer hours. Which means they spend their hard-earned money enjoying themselves later into the evening. Which means they have much less time to read books anywhere else except in the only place where their cell phones don't work and no one is likely to know them or talk to them.

Many subway riders, like David Gassawy, a 29-year-old art teacher, see their commute as the best uninterrupted reading time remaining in their lives, one not to be squandered on newspapers or magazines.

Spending a long morning watching people read on the subway, one can learn a few general principles about the practice. Mr. Gassawy expounded the first one yesterday: fiction is superior subway reading. "Nonfiction is more work—it's harder to do it on the subway," he said. "Maybe it's something about following a narrative in fiction." (Mr. Gassawy was on a southbound A train, reading something called "The War of Don Emmanuel's Nether Parts," by Louis De Bernieres, a novel in which one character builds a Disneyland in the Andes called Incarama.)

Another general guideline is that people tend to have their subway books and then they have the books they are reading elsewhere. Rarely do the two libraries mingle.

Michelle Mills, a 25-year-old design student, well into Book Two of "The Lord of the Rings," by J. R. R. Tolkien, said, "If I'm really, *really* into a book then I might keep reading it at home to finish it." But mostly, she puts away her subway book as she steps out of the train doors and yearns for a longer commute, something other reading riders admitted to yesterday. "If your ride is too short," Ms. Mills explained, "then you keep losing the story every day."

There is, finally, a widespread phenomenon that might be classified as subway book bashfulness. It happens when people who usually read Kierkegaard at home read King (as in Stephen) on the subway, and become so self-conscious that they fold the title page back or hold the front of the book firmly down in their laps. It also happens in reverse, when readers like Mr. Gassawy get the urge to read something as chewy and highbrow as "The Society of the Spectacle," by the French theorist Guy Debord. "I covered it up with a paper jacket," he admitted. "I had to. I just felt too pretentious holding that up in the subway."

Of course, some readers are much too into their prose to worry about etiquette. Brad Audett, working on his master's degree at John Jay College of Criminal Justice, was concentrating yesterday on "Without Conscience: The Disturbing World of the Psychopaths Among Us," by Robert D. Hare. Some fellow riders were staring.

"I read a lot of books about serial killers," he said. "It's what I'm studying at school."

"I don't really notice, but I guess it does freak some people out."

—ORIGINALLY PUBLISHED NOVEMBER 7, 2000

LEG-SPREADERS

Gillian Costello is a lawyer. Proof is important to her. So yesterday, to show a reporter something on the subway, she conducted a simple empirical demonstration.

Ms. Costello had absolutely no doubt about the outcome of her experiment, because she tests this particular hypothesis twice every workday. As do most women in New York, whenever they manage to get a seat on a crowded train. The hypothesis: Men take up a lot more room on the subway than women. They stretch out. They lean. They do the Ward Cleaver ankle-on-knee leg cross. But mostly, and most damnably, they tend to sit with their legs splayed out like catchers behind home plate.

And sitting next to them will invariably be a woman like Ms. Costello—knees clamped together, shoulders hunched, bag on lap and newspaper folded into a thin column, hiding a face with the pained expression peculiar to someone who is being touched by a total stranger over a long period of time.

Her demonstration began yesterday morning at 9:30 at the Bergen Street station in Brooklyn, where Ms. Costello, 35, catches the No. 2 train every morning. Crowding in the cars was light, and Ms. Costello got lucky, wedged in between a woman and what seemed to be an anomalous man, his feet only shoulder-width apart.

But before the train had gone two stops, she spotted several grievous examples of the transgression. "Look at that guy," she said, pointing toward a small man wearing a backpack the size of a compact car. The man sat down with the backpack still on, ramming it into several people. And then, as if he had not made his presence sufficiently felt, he butterflied his knees into the passengers on both sides.

Ms. Costello shook her head. "He's guilty of several offenses," she said.

Next was the very, very big guy down the bench with the black beret and the flowing beard who was not only spread-eagled but sound asleep and swaying from side to side like a boxer in the 15th round.

Then there was the young guy sitting on a two-person bench at the end of the car. His elbows were on his knees and his knees were spread out so far that no one even tried to sit next to him.

"That's not just invading space," Ms. Costello said, framing her arguments carefully, as if for a judge. "That's foreclosing on it altogether."

When the topic of the Encroaching Male is raised among women at her law firm or at a party, Ms. Costello says, it becomes a kind of rallying cry. It ranks high on the list of subway irritants, up there with people who stand in the door, people who push into the train before letting others off and people who lean their entire bodies against the poles (making it impossible for anyone else to use them to hang on).

But these other offenses sometimes cross gender lines. Space invasion, on the other hand, tends to be one in which women are almost without sin and so they can cast imaginary stones—right into the crotches of their offenders.

There are several theories about why it happens, all of them gross generalizations. Women sit with their legs together more often because they are wearing skirts or because they were taught that sitting that way is more becoming. Men sit the way they sit because they think keeping their legs together looks prim or because they are compelled by a primordial instinct left over from the days when they sat on tree limbs and had to make themselves look bigger so something would not come along and eat them.

Ms. Costello thinks there may be something to the latter theory: "It does tend to be the leaner guys who spread themselves out even more."

Of course, there are always exceptions, like the large woman in the leopard-print pants sitting next to Ms. Costello on the C train, whose knee spread beat all the men on the seat. But exceptions are rare.

Even rarer is the man who recognizes that he is guilty.

Eugene Lareau, a 56-year-old messenger, was one of the men who impinged on Ms. Costello's space yesterday. As she left the train, a reporter asked Mr. Lareau what he thought about her lament.

"I don't know why people do that," he said, oblivious to the fact that he had just done it. "I guess the subway brings out the worst in people."

—ORIGINALLY PUBLISHED NOVEMBER 14, 2000

TOKEN PEOPLE

They are creatures of habit. They are harborers of history. They don't trust technology. They frustrate economic theorists, refusing to change their behavior in exchange for a bargain.

In the language of marketing, they are known as the non-adapters.

The rest of us can think of them as the token people.

And they are a dying breed, one that knows its days are numbered. New York City Transit reported last month that MetroCard users now represent more than 81 percent of the fare-paying public. The agency also said recently that within the next two years it expected to start phasing out tokens, which have served as tiny relics of the true New York since the first ones were minted in 1953.

Most people with reservations about switching have already put them aside in the seven years since the MetroCard was introduced.

But the token people, like the last old settlers to come down from the hills, are the ones who say they will hold out until the last token slot is welded shut.

"Other people can do what they want to do," said Jimmy Harris, a 50-year-old porter, who grew almost defiant the other day at the Times Square subway station when asked why he does not use MetroCards. "I like tokens, that's why," he said.

All around them, the token people have seen their friends and coworkers slowly lose that certain jingle in their pockets. Of course, this switch has not always been easy for the millions who have made it. Staking out a token booth for a couple of hours, one can still detect a high level of affection for the token, an affection that seems mostly to do with urban practicality.

Flimsy cards can get bent. They can get lost in wallets, wallets that must be pulled out and exposed to thieves while lost cards are being fumbled for. The cards can also lose their magnetic mojo or require you to swipe them 10 times. But unless you happen to get caught in a metal press on your way to the turnstile your token will always work.

The other benefit to the token in many riders' minds is that it requires no math. One token equals one ride. It does not offer a discount, but it will also never be hiding an extra ride within it somewhere that you have forgotten about.

M. A. Horn, a credit manager, really, really did not want to switch. And he's still quite angry about it. "They forced me to do it," he complained the other day outside a Times Square turnstile. "And they force me to buy lots of trips. If I don't, then I'm passing up free trips. And then I'm a fool." (Mr. Horn has clearly spent too much time thinking about this. He called a reporter later to explain that he had calculated that a penniless homeless person would have to redeem 300 bottles or cans to gather enough money to purchase a $15 MetroCard, the cheapest card that offers a volume discount. "Think of that!" Mr. Horn said.)

Norman Siegel, a civil liberties lawyer, did not want to switch either. Like everyone else, he gave in mostly because of the discounts. But he still does not use a credit card when he buys his MetroCard. And he still worries, every time he stands before a MetroCard machine, about the ability of the government to track people who use the card.

"I don't want them knowing where I'm going, even though I'm as innocent as anyone in the city and as lawful as anyone in the city," he said. "And you don't have to be paranoid to think that way."

Many of the true token people feel the same way, except they will not be bought off so easily by discounts.

Carlos Fernandez, 23, a senior at the State University of New York in Purchase, reported by e-mail that when he tried out the Metro-Card, he felt as if he were entering a kind of government-controlled

"Area 51, where every little bit of information and detail is scrutinized."

In his message, he added, "Who will be there to open the gate manually when the M.T.A. computers befall a belated Y2K? In the era of online hackers, one can never be too certain."

Nick Liopiros, a waiter, is among that rarest of token people, one who has never even tried a MetroCard. "Forty-one years in city, only token," he said. "This MetroCard, no. Never." He added, "With me is strong habit."

But that might be changing. Mr. Liopiros was asked if he felt a certain amount of pride in stubbornly passing up the discounts offered by the MetroCard. His countenance quickly changed. He leaned his stubbly face in close to the questioner.

"They give discount?"

—ORIGINALLY PUBLISHED FEBRUARY 6, 2001

DON'T DARKEN MY DOORWAY

Honestly, it was not with malice, but in the true spirit of psychological inquiry—think of it as Freud on the F train—that a reporter set out yesterday morning to ask the following questions of a particular subset of subway riders:

Why do you like to ride standing in the doorway of the train? Even when there are lots of nice, comfortable seats available? And why do you insist on remaining planted right in the middle of the doorway when the doors open in the station, forcing people to squeeze around you to get into the train?

They are questions that many subway riders would love to ask themselves, of course, but they don't have the excuse of writing a newspaper column, so they are afraid they might get punched. The column writer was a little afraid of this himself, but he figured that the subject of door blockers ranked so high on anyone's list of subway irritants that the risk should be taken. (Besides, he had a 6-foot-5 photographer to back him up.)

Gene Russianoff, of the Straphangers Campaign, the advocacy group for riders, says that willful door blocking has been a consistently enraging phenomenon as long as he can remember. Once at a public forum, he said, a rider only half-jokingly suggested to transit officials that new subway trains should come equipped with tiny, sharp stakes that would shoot up in the doorway area as soon as the doors closed, so that no one could stand there without puncturing a foot.

Transit officials demurred. They did, however, propose designing new subway cars with a generous recess next to the doorway, so that standers might have a pocket all to themselves, slightly out of the doorway. But the plan would have meant fewer seats—and in the world of the subway, where nearly every addition requires subtraction, seats ended up a higher priority than sanity. (New trains being tested now have a recess of only about 6 inches, and yesterday, every door blocker interviewed was much wider than that.)

As his luck would have it, Eddy Colon, 42, became the first subject of yesterday's survey. Mr. Colon was spotted on the No. 4 train at Grand Central in the familiar stance, the one seared into many riders' brains: feet slightly apart, squarely in the middle of the door, one hand on the metal handle, back to the platform as the doors slid open. It seemed that everything in the subway was moving except Mr. Colon.

Five people trying to get into the train had to wait while the four people trying to get out turned sideways past Mr. Colon. Then the people getting on wiggled around him, being careful not to touch him or the gold "#1" medallion hanging around his neck. ("You don't want to touch them," said Frantz Malcousu, 47, an electronics technician from Brooklyn, when asked about door blockers yesterday at Times Square. "You never know what kind of mood a guy is going to be in.")

As it turned out, Mr. Colon was not in the best mood. He was asked if he was aware he was making some people unhappy. He said he did not understand the question. It was rephrased, cautiously. He said he still didn't understand, and then he started to smile, in a way that did not make a reporter feel like Mr. Colon thought anything was funny.

Finally, he shrugged and said, unconvincingly, "This is the first time I ever rode the subway. I don't know what you're supposed to do."

Jerome D'Aguiar, a conductor, says his favorite blockers are ones who remain fully in everyone's way at the edge of the door and then lean out when the doors open and look suspiciously up and down the platform, as if they are spies trying to shake a tail.

"I never can figure out what they're looking for," Mr. D'Aguiar said.

Mr. D'Aguiar is 6-foot-5. He has a big Grizzly Adams beard. He can get away with asking door blockers if they would care to step a little further into the train. But he advises others simply to make themselves skinny and practice the part of valor that is supposed to be the better part.

He said that people who give door blockers a nice, hard shoulder check on the way out of the train—on the theory that the guy (it is almost always a guy) won't get off his train to exact retribution—are playing a dangerous game.

"I've seen some guys get off the train," he said. "These are people *wanting* to have a confrontation.

"If you let it get to you," he added, "you're going to be having a confrontation every day."

A reporter took the advice to heart but felt compelled to seek out a few more confrontations. He quickly found the next one on an uptown C train, where a man walked into a car at Times Square with a short line of people behind him. As soon as he cleared the threshold, he stopped and planted himself and the line had to snake around him.

"There's two doors here, see," the man explained later, when approached. "I'm only standing in front of one."

A little later, he added, "It's America. I can stand wherever I want."

When asked to spell his name, he smiled—that smile again. "Joe Blow. B-L-O-W."

—ORIGINALLY PUBLISHED MAY 22, 2001

LOVE AND PROSECUTIONS

Among places for making a romantic connection, the New York City subway has long ranked down around the bottom of the list, just above jail or the proctologist's office.

But along with the drop in crime, the rise in subway cleanliness and the herds of new riders who have discovered the trains over the last few years, there are signs that the subway as singles scene may also be having a renaissance. (The subway was once considered a place of romance, after all. Think of "On the Town," in which Gene Kelly spotted the love of his life on a subway beauty-contest poster.)

Examples of public transportation's newfound sexiness seem to be all over the place. A new television commercial in which a gang of D.J.'s commandeer a subway car and turn it into a dance club. Another in which a subway motorwoman stops her train to remark on the nice pants worn by the guy in the next train over. An article on the Web magazine Salon last year in which the writer bragged about how she and her friends were "collecting so many phone numbers on the subway these days."

This column began looking for a way to tap into this phenomenon, but it was a little too awkward to interview people in the middle of hitting on each other. So it was decided that the best way would be to solicit letters from friends and acquaintances recounting their true tales of finding—or, alas, losing—love on the subway.

Dear **Tunnel Vision**:

A good friend and I decided that reckless date-finding measures were in order, and so, on a mutual dare, we agreed that we would each accost and arrange a date with at least one stranger on the N.Y.C. subway. I was soon equipped with a business card on which I had written, "I swear I've never done this before, but call me?"

I never used the card because I ditched it after nearly passing it out at several important business meetings. Luckily, I was shortly thereafter caught kibbitzing on the platform at West Fourth Street by a woman more reckless than I. She had been ribbing her friend and noticed by my smirks that I admired her wit. The three of us began a jovial banter, and as I prepared to disembark at 23rd Street, the witty ribber said, "So how will my friend ever find you again?" I promptly produced a business card—undoctored—and slipped it into the friend's hand. Half an hour later I checked my voice mail and already there was a raucous message from the two of them, including a phone number for the promising ribbee.

She was only briefly promising, however, as subsequent communications revealed the existence of a "boyfriend" who, for whatever reason, had not merited previous mention.

Still, not bad for the subway. And, since it's essentially true, I now have another business card that says "I swear I've never done this before . . ."

ROBERT WOOD
Economist, 34

Dear **Tunnel Vision**:

I was on a train coming back home to Brooklyn and, at the Broadway-Lafayette station, I noticed a man who got on and sat near me. He was probably 19 or 20. I am 35, married and a mother. There was nothing flirtatious going on. You know how you get on the train and pick out those people who you think would be the ones who would help you if someone started to rob you? That's what I thought about this guy.

But as I started to get off, he jumped up and ran after me. I thought I had dropped something, but he handed me a card that said, "Clean-cut kid." With a phone number. (Actually, he didn't look very clean-cut. Maybe it's a generational thing.)

The card also said his name was Ben. Apparently, he was feeling a little Mrs. Robinson about me.

SARA GOODMAN

Film company employee, 35

Dear **Tunnel Vision**:

I was clutching at a string of hope. My boyfriend of six months, a lawyer, had just spent the night at my apartment. Now, on our walk to the Borough Hall train station, I was pondering things. Sure, we had our share of troubles, but we had fun together, and we had grown close over time. I was dreaming of a future.

But as the No. 4 train came screeching into the station, he was weighing the evidence: his idea of a holiday is Rollerblading across the country; mine is floating in tropical waters. His day at the beach is a triathlon; mine is a clambake. He is an exhibitionist; I am an extremely private person. As the car doors tried to close for the ninth time, he prepared his opening statement. An elbow jammed into my kidney as he listed the pros and cons of our relationship out loud. I heard a stomach grumbling behind me. I smelled someone's chewing gum.

Seemingly unaware of the commuters crushing around us, he kept building his case, telling me the reasons why it would never work out.

When he had convinced himself, he didn't bother with a closing statement. The No. 4 pulled into City Hall. As my boyfriend got off the train, he became my ex-boyfriend. I'd been prosecuted.

ANNA KOVEL
Chef, 35

—ORIGINALLY PUBLISHED JUNE 12, 2001

CHEAP SWEETENERS

If you keep an eye on other subways around the world, you'll detect what could be a strange new trend in public transit.

It appears to have come about like this: ridership is growing in nearly every city in the world that has a subway system. But the systems, which require unthinkable sums of money to build, are not growing nearly as rapidly. So what are poor transit officials to do, beset on one side by their budgets and on the other by several billion sweaty, crowded riders who are late to work and looking for someone to blame? The answer is to try very, very hard to be nice. Maybe it will work, and if not, at least it doesn't cost much.

Early this year in Paris, where the subway is one hundred years old and suffering from strikes as well as delays and other signs of age, the powers came up with a typically French fix: let them have massages. And—bien sûr!—food. The company that operates the city's Metro put up posters at four stations that said nice, soothing things like "Let's be Zen." And then, as rush-hour crowds pushed by, they offered riders free 10-minute massages—choose from eight different styles—plus green tea and seaweed crackers to send them on their way.

Down the road, Stockholm's version was not quite as fancy but much funnier. The company that runs the city's subway, Connex Tunnelbanan, hired "laughing instructors" last month to go into the subways and help riders see the funny side of being overcrowded. "They join the people on the tube and explain to them why laughter is such a good thing," said a company spokeswoman, who seemed to find nothing particularly humorous about the idea.

This column set out yesterday afternoon to figure out what kinds of cheap sweeteners New York subway riders would like to see while they wait for the Second Avenue subway to be built. (They have been waiting since about 1920, when it was first proposed.)

Grand Central Terminal was chosen for the survey because it is arguably the most crowded station on the most crowded line in the city, the Lexington. And, as one might expect, people there thought that some free stuff was long overdue.

"I want the back rubs, and I want the clowns," said Noah Johnson, a construction foreman, sweating as he waited for a train. "Right now, I have a little time, and I would love to go get a back massage."

Like the most thoughtful of those interviewed, Mr. Johnson, 50, was not wasting his wishes to this would-be genie. Snacks were no good, he said, because they would attract homeless people and then "you couldn't eat because of the body odor."

Others were not quite so practical. There were requests for free hot dogs, to be dispensed by workers on the platforms. For gift bags—with bottles of spring water, maybe, and free magazines and little samples of hand lotion. For battery-powered face fans and booze and televisions on the platforms showing all wrestling, all the time.

"A sweet cookie ain't bad," said Ted Williams, preparing to play some Delta blues on his guitar. "A cookie that says M.T.A. on it.

SUBWAYLAND

People would like that." He also mentioned tickets to the Maury Povich show, but then remembered they were free anyway.

Esaú Gutierrez, a cook sitting nearby, figured why stop there. "Entradas para los juegos," he said, meaning tickets to the games, meaning, specifically, Yankees games. He smiled at the thought.

Gene Russianoff, the staff lawyer for the Straphangers Campaign, had a few ideas that he thought would be even more fun for everyone—except maybe for one guy. He proposed a weekly outdoor gaming event called "Dunk a Transit President," in which "the president of the Transit Authority would go to the Coney Island/Stillwell Avenue subway station. Riders could blow off steam from their long, slow, crowded trip to the ocean by throwing tokens at an M.T.A. 'Going Your Way' logo; bull's-eyes would result in dunking the president in an aquarium of refreshing New York seawater."

Al O'Leary, a spokesman for the Transit Authority, did not comment on the merits of this idea. But he did point out that the agency sponsored the Music Under New York program to bring nice, sometimes soothing music into the subway. And it has placed all sorts of nice, beautiful artworks in newly renovated stations. And it posts nice, encouraging poems in the trains, like this one by Ogden Nash:

> Let each man haste to indulge his taste,
> Be it beer, champagne or cider;
> My private joy, both man and boy,
> Is being a railroad rider.

"I can't say there's been any proactive effort to increase the number of yucks on hot, crowded subway stations," Mr. O'Leary said. "But New Yorkers are capable of finding the humor in a lot of things. For example, those 20-year-old guys who are panhandling and say they were in Vietnam. I think New Yorkers find those guys funny."

—ORIGINALLY PUBLISHED JULY 17, 2001

FUNERAL AT SEA

With a splash instead of a screech, Redbird subway car No. 7835 made its last stop today.

It was born around 1959 in Berwick, Pa. It spent more than 40 years under and above the streets of New York, carrying far more than a million passengers within its bloodred-painted steel walls. And at 1:08 p.m., it toppled ingloriously over the edge of a rusty barge off the coast of Delaware, traveling 80 feet to its final resting place, where its new passengers, all nonpaying, will be blue mussels and black sea bass.

The cause of death, according to New York City Transit, was old age and the high cost of maintenance.

"Goodbye, Dr. Zizmor, forever," said David Ross, the transit official who had the slightly crazy idea last year that maybe the agency could junk its oldest subway cars more cheaply by dumping them in the ocean to serve as artificial reefs.

It was not the first scheme that had been proposed for scrapping 1,300 rusting, rattling cars, known as Redbirds, which are being retired over the next two years as a sleek new generation of trains begins to replace them. Because the old cars contain a layer of asbestos within their walls for sound and heat insulation, tearing them apart for junk metal would have involved a costly process of asbestos removal.

So transit officials first explored the idea of donating the cars to a somewhat needier subway system. They literally called around the world, talking to Romania, Hungary, China, Brazil, India, Pakistan and Turkey, but figured out that it was far from simple, legally and diplomatically, to give away an 80,000-pound, asbestos-spiked subway car.

Even after the reef idea was broached, finding a nice stretch of ocean floor for the cars was not easy. In April, New Jersey officials rejected the idea for their waters, citing uncertainty about how quickly the cars would deteriorate under the water and possibly allow the asbestos to contaminate sea life.

But in June, the Delaware Department of Natural Resources and Environmental Control accepted the idea, and agreed to take four hundred cars, after assurances from the United States Environmental Protection Agency that interments at sea were safe.

Today, 27 of the weathered cars were lined up like condemned inmates along the deck of a marine salvage barge that heaved to about 19 miles east of Cape Henlopen, Del. The cars, which had been loaded onto the barge in a train yard in Manhattan Thursday, had been stripped of their wheels, motors, seats and the window glass—even the infamous Dr. Zizmor acne ads.

But most of the metal straps upon which generations of straphangers hung remained on board. The reef, Delaware officials explained, needed as many hard surfaces as possible to create "an enriched invertebrate community" where once a tense, overcrowded New Yorker community had thrived.

As funerals go, the subway sea burial was less than solemn. Reef advocates and state legislators watched from a nearby ferry, sipping champagne and chewing on roast beef sandwiches, as the cars plunked one by one into the water, where they would soon be keeping silent company with two sunken tugboats and a barge.

Before the first car took its dive, officials from New York and Delaware held a simple ceremony aboard the ferry to commemorate the occasion. The Rev. Capt. Thomas J. Protack of the Delaware Division of Fish and Wildlife Enforcement asked God's blessing on the subway cars and the new reef they would form. "May it be a place where your creatures can dwell in peace and safety," he prayed.

A former New Yorker, Blackie Nygood, led about one hundred people onboard the ferry in a rousing rendition of "The Sidewalks of New York." Then, right before a yellow bulldozer shoved the first Redbird off into the drink, Mrs. Nygood cast three subway tokens upon the water—one for the IRT subway line, one for the BMT and the last for the IND.

At least one transit official considered all of this a lucky omen and called a friend on his cell phone to have him buy a lottery ticket bearing the number of the first car to go overboard. "Dollar straight, dollar box," he said into the phone.

Bill Baker, owner of Bill's Sport Shop in Lewes, Del., was not just hoping to get lucky. He knew he would: he sells tackle. More reefs mean more fish. More fish mean more fishermen. More fishermen mean more business.

Bill Weiss, who works at the shop, said, "You know how many more sinkers we're going to sell?"

Mr. Baker thought about it. "This is the biggest thing that's happened in Delaware in a hundred years."

—ORIGINALLY PUBLISHED AUGUST 22, 2001

SONG OF THE SUBWAY

Pretty much since trains started rolling, people have been fascinated with the sounds they make. Songs have been inspired by the rhythm of the engine ("Orange Blossom Special"), the dirge of the whistle ("I Heard That Lonesome Whistle"), even the thunder of the crash ("Wreck of the Old '97").

As lyrical as they are considered to be, however, trains themselves are not known for making music.

So a few months back, when riders on the No. 2 line began to hear an ethereal song, or at least the opening strain to one, emanating from the newest generation of silvery subway trains, they almost distrusted themselves.

Roy Futterman, a clinical psychologist who commutes from the Upper West Side to the Bronx, was reminded of a psychotic symptom called ideas of reference, in which, for example, the sufferer watches an episode of "Happy Days," and believes that the Fonz is delivering a message directly to him.

"I'm riding the subway, and I keep hearing this song," Dr. Futterman said. "And I think: Am I having an idea of reference? Am *I* getting the secret message?"

If he was, he was not the only one. Lots of people, especially when they were standing around the middle of the new subway trains, swore they could hear three distinct, electric-sounding high notes coming from somewhere on the trains after their doors were closed and the trains began to pull away.

It was definitely not the same, boring whirr of the older trains, which starts low and slowly builds to a resounding high note, like a bad Jennifer Holliday impersonator. It was not the ding-dong of the doors, which is already burned deeply into every brain cell of the regular subway rider. This sounded more futuristic, like something from a Philip Glass opera, the last note trailing off magisterially.

Having nothing more interesting to do than dread work or angle for a seat or pretend to read, riders on the line have begun to pass their time by trying to figure out what song it is and, more importantly, why it is being played.

There are the theremin partisans, who swear that the sound is the eerie electronic one you hear in countless science-fiction movies, usually played as the alien descends from the mother ship. Others say it sounds like the three-note NBC theme, but most agree that the notes are not quite that upbeat.

Lately, a strong consensus seems to be building around the notes being the first three from "Somewhere" in "West Side Story"—the ones that go with the words "There's a place." This does make some strange sense: the No. 2 runs through the mythical turf of the Sharks and Jets. (The only argument against the theory are the words that come later in the verse, which have no place in the subway: "Peace and quiet and open air.")

Figuring out why New York City subway trains seem to be playing Leonard Bernstein proves a much more difficult task. Juan Harvey, a messenger waiting yesterday at the 66th Street station, said he has heard the song and believes it is "some kind of a plot by the Japanese to brainwash us all."

This would be an intriguing line of inquiry, except that the new No. 2 trains are actually manufactured by a Canadian company called Bombardier. Informed of this, Mr. Harvey said that he did not think the Canadians would want to brainwash us.

A call was placed to the engineers at Bombardier in Plattsburgh, N.Y., where the trains are assembled. All questions about musical trains were referred to someone named Andre, who could not take the call and did not return it yesterday.

So a reporter went to a meeting at the headquarters of the Metropolitan Transportation Authority on Madison Avenue, hoping to find answers there. Joseph Hofmann, the senior vice president for subways, professed never to have heard the song but said that if it were up to him, it would certainly not be anything from "West Side Story." He was once an usher at a production of the musical and listened to all its songs at least two hundred times.

"Don't talk to me about 'West Side Story,'" he said.

The question was put next to George Feinstein, the transit

agency's project manager for the new trains, who said the explanation most likely was a mundane one, having to do with the advanced engines of the new trains, which use alternating instead of direct current, as older trains do. The direct current from the third rail is converted aboard the train to alternating current, and in the process, perhaps, beautiful music is made.

"I don't think anybody planned it that way," said Mr. Feinstein, shattering the illusions of Dr. Futterman, who had hoped there was a mad transit genius out there somewhere who said to himself, "Hmmm. I've got to let the air out of this gadget one way or another. Why don't I build it so that when it does, it plays a nice little song?"

—ORIGINALLY PUBLISHED JANUARY 29, 2002

THE G-TRAIN SPRINT

New York has bestowed names on many things over the years. There is the New York minute and the Bronx cheer, the Manhattan cocktail and the Waldorf salad. Even Mount Rushmore is named after a New Yorker, Charles E. Rushmore, a lawyer who owned mining property in the area.

There is now a chance that a new fitness routine will be named for something that has been happening spontaneously at subway stations in Brooklyn and Queens over the last four months. Locally, it has become known as the G-train sprint.

The basic workout goes like this: Warm up by walking through a turnstile carrying your bag and a cup of hot deli coffee. When you hear a beeping sound that means a train is approaching, start to jog toward the stairway.

Upon reaching the middle of the stairs and seeing that the train is much shorter than you thought it would be, therefore farther away, bound down the stairs two at a time, exercising your vocal chords by making panic-like sounds. Once on the platform, break into a full sprint, dodging or ramming, if necessary, the people who are getting off the train and walking in the opposite direction.

This routine is intended to work most major muscle groups, develop cardiovascular strength and improve coordination. After enough practice, you should be able to jump into the end car of the shortened train just as the doors close on your bag, splashing only a little coffee on your shirt. Do not be discouraged if you cannot perform the exercise correctly on the first few tries.

Joan Dougherty, a paralegal, was not able to do it yesterday morning at the Greenpoint Avenue station, and she has been training there for months. She complained grievously of a violation of the rules. "The guy saw me!" she said of the conductor, as his train pulled out and he watched with a bored expression as her sprint faded to a jog.

Peter Jou, a computer programmer, decided not to try at all. From the top of the stairs, he saw the train, paused and then walked calmly and evenly down as it pulled away. "I'm always afraid I'm going to fall down the stairs," he explained.

The situation that has given rise to the G-train sprint is part of a series of Solomonic bargains, the kind that New York City Transit must make when it tries to change anything within the rigid logic of the subway.

In order to reduce crushing crowding in Queens, it added the V train along Queens Boulevard, where the E, F, R and G already ran. But that meant too many trains for too few tracks, so one train had to go, and it ended up being the G, which had its route cut almost in half. Of course, an uproar ensued among its riders. And so a concession was made: the train would continue to run its full route weekends and nights, and it would also run more frequently, particularly during busy times.

Except there was another problem. To run more frequently, the

G needed more trains, but there were not enough on hand. So the solution was to cut the trains from six cars to four, sticking all the leftover cars together to make extra trains. While on paper this means more trains, it seems to riders that it means only more of them, packed into smaller trains.

And, more importantly for explaining the G-train sprint, it means that on a platform designed to be filled by an eight-car, 600-foot train, the ones that show up now are only 300 feet long. Back in December, when the change was first made, paper signs were posted on platform columns to let riders know where these truncated trains would stop. But the signs are gone now and for people unfamiliar with the line, the wind sprints have begun.

"I was at Bergen Street one day, and it looked like the burning of Atlanta in 'Gone With the Wind,'" said Gene Russianoff, a lawyer for the Straphangers Campaign who lives along the G line in Brooklyn. "There were all these people flooding down the platform in waves."

Patti Choi, a member of the Noble Street Block Association in Greenpoint, has been riding the G train so long she remembers when it was called something else. She looked imploringly at a conductor yesterday as a few of the weaker runners barely managed to make his train at the Greenpoint Avenue station. The conductor shrugged as the train pulled away. "I waited for them, right?" he said. "You saw me waiting."

Eddy Rodriguez and John Marshall barely made it. Before the train came, they had been chewing the fat on a bench that was a relic of a more genteel past: The trains don't stop there anymore.

"You write down this: 'We want our train back,'" said Mr. Rodriguez, wearing a jacket with the word "Bulldog" written in capital letters on the back, running down the platform with a cup of coffee and a bad limp. "Did you write that down?"

—ORIGINALLY PUBLISHED APRIL 9, 2002

RIDING FOR TWO

It is a familiar refrain that September 11 showed not only the world but even New Yorkers themselves how nice they could really be. They gave time and money and food. They gave Caribbean cruises to firefighters. They gave rides to perfect strangers trying to get home that horrible day.

But a recent impromptu investigation has found that there is still at least one thing most New Yorkers will not give to anyone, under any circumstances, even in this renaissance of compassion: a seat on a crowded subway train.

To conduct the investigation, a suitable seat-seeker was quickly found: Rebecca Hunter, 32, Brooklynite, professional woman and proud subway rider who also happens to be seven months pregnant and among the most extremely uncomfortable of the uncomfortable riders on the F, A and C trains, the three Ms. Hunter takes to work in the West Village.

Over the last seven months, Ms. Hunter's sense of subway topography has changed with each trimester, and to see the system through her eyes now is to see it much differently. It is to realize that there are no air-conditioning vents near the ends of F train cars, so that even when it is less crowded there, Ms. Hunter gets on in the middle, where it is cooler.

It is to notice that there are few benches on the long platforms at the Jay Street station in Brooklyn, and that the F comes into West Fourth Street in Manhattan two levels down, a long hike for a woman carrying far more than a briefcase.

Most of all, though, it is to understand the casual lack of courtesy on rush-hour trains, badly hidden behind newspapers, novels and supposedly sleepy eyelids.

Ms. Hunter, an Internet producer, said she did not mind it when she was less far along. She would see sympathetic people

149

looking at her nervously and she knew what they were thinking: "Is she pregnant or does she just need to lay off the burgers?"

Later on, though, as her midsection grew and her feet began to ache, she would wrinkle her nose politely at someone staring and mouth the words, "Yes, I am pregnant," longing for the seat.

Now, there is no mistaking, and no excuses remain for those sitting around her. "Sometimes," she says, "people will have conversations with me when they're sitting and they'll say, 'So, how far along are you?' and I'm thinking, 'I'm far enough along that you should get up!'"

Ms. Hunter, who came to New York from Boston by way of Arizona two years ago, does not think that a seat is her right, the way it should be for the disabled and the elderly. She simply thinks it is a nice thing for people to give her. She did it before she was pregnant. Her husband, David, does it.

At 8:30 the other morning on the F train from Brooklyn, no one was doing it.

There was a young man hunched intently over a loud electronic game. There was a young woman hunched intently over the novel "Me Times Three," oddly appropriate because that is the way Ms. Hunter feels right now.

There was another man who looked promising. "He looked like he might have been a hippie in college and maybe he had some feminist leanings," Ms. Hunter said later. As it turned out, he had no such leanings. She rode for four stations—conspicuously turning her prominent abdomen, draped in a bright pink shirt. Finally someone got up, but only to leave the train.

Over the last weeks, Ms. Hunter has made her own accounting of subway politeness, complete with percentages. A quarter of the time, someone gives her a seat, like the nice young woman with the cat glasses last Thursday morning. A quarter of the time, she gets a seat through dumb luck or "through my own cunning"—watching for vacancies and positioning herself like a bobcat crouched for prey. Half the time, there are no seats and no offers.

Ms. Hunter says that on the lines she rides from her neighborhood, Windsor Terrace, women make up 90 percent of the seat-givers, and young Hispanic men are also very generous. By and large, everyone else falls into the category of great disappointment.

Standing, she longs to hear these people's internal rationalizations, and recently she did, sort of. In a subway chat room, there was a discussion of subway etiquette in which a man who called himself Davy opined that pregnant women should not be riding crowded trains anyway.

Ms. Hunter showed considerable restraint in her response. "Let's see. Why do I ride the train at such a crowded time?" she wrote. "Because I have a job. Because in order to live in this city, my husband and I both need jobs." She added, "Do you have a job where you can just come and go as you please? If so, please do me a favor and pass my résumé along."

Yesterday morning, standing, on the way to her job where she cannot come and go as she pleases, she said she had made a new resolution.

"I am going to start asking people to get up," she said. "I've decided."

—ORIGINALLY PUBLISHED APRIL 30, 2002

POLE-HUGGERS

Of the many breaches of that vast, elaborate and unwritten code of conduct known as the Rules of New York City Subway Etiquette, pole-hugging has long been lumped among the lesser offenses.

It certainly does not deserve the kind of high-pitched and near-violent censure set aside for door blockers, those who ride in doorways and move for no one. It is not nearly as willful as rush-ing (entering a car before riders inside can exit) or as oblivious as stopping (entering a car and lingering at the threshold, while dozens behind you try to get in). In the end, its consequences are probably not as serious as either leg-spreading (riders, mostly men, sitting like catchers behind home plate) or bag-sitting (riders, mostly women, storing their recent purchases on the seat next to them).

But there seems to be a growing movement among subway etiquette jurists—or at least among the dozen or so people who were recently found at random on trains across the city and interviewed—that a reclassification of pole-hugging may be in order.

Properly defined, of course, pole-hugging is one of two subcate-gories under the general offense of pole-hogging, which also includes pole-leaning. But the results are the same: the vertical poles inside subway cars, intended to be gripped by as many as five or six hands on a crowded train, are instead monopolized by one body, which tends to be large and perspiring heavily. Often, the body is reading a newspaper and leaning against the pole as if it were in a small-town barbershop. Sometimes, the body wraps the pole in its arms like an old waltzing partner. Occasionally, the body is doing the one-armed hug or the one-shoulder lean—less serious but still taking up wildly undemocratic amounts of pole space.

It could be that trains are much more crowded now, and pole space is at a premium. It could be that the offense of pole-hugging, overlooked for so many years, has simply grown unchecked. What-ever the reason, the consensus is that it should be discouraged much more vigorously, and that there are many ways to do it.

Aida Melendez favors the wrist method, considered one of the best. The hand is inserted between the pole and the offender firmly, and then the wrist is given a hard snap to cause discomfort to the offender. "It's passive-aggressive, like everything in the subway," said Ms. Melendez, a nurse from Park Slope, Brooklyn. "Except it's more aggressive than passive."

She added that if the offender still does not budge, she adds the additional and sometimes effective technique of "sucking my teeth and rolling my eyes."

Large rings, bracelets and watches make the wrist method even more effective. But Stephanie Leveene, an editor who rides the N, R, 4 and 5 trains, counsels that true opponents of pole-huggers must be willing to go the distance with them. "They don't want the hand in their back," she said. "But sometimes they won't move and I won't move, and we just ride like that, all the way."

"I will," she added, proudly, "put up with a back on my hand if I have to." (She and Ms. Melendez are both short and point out that short people hate pole-huggers even more because the horizontal handrails are usually too high for short people to hang onto comfortably.)

Tom Range, a retired accountant who rode the crowded E and F lines for 30 years and won many battles with pole-huggers, said he relied on a briefcase corner in the kidney area, followed by a very sincere-sounding apology.

Raymond Tatti, a computer network engineer, favors a less direct method. He will reach up and put his hand on the pole above the offender's head, menacingly. Others counsel reaching for the mid-section if the hugger is facing you, but this should be used with extreme caution because some huggers may be looking for exactly this sort of interaction.

As you might expect, pole-huggers and leaners tend not to be the types of people who like to explain themselves. Last Friday morning, on an R train in downtown Brooklyn, a tall, pudgy man was leaned against a pole, touching it from his rear end to the top of his head. He was pursued out of the train, where he declined an interview. "I am not interested in participating," he said nervously, putting his headphones back on.

Aldo Medina, at the 23rd Street station on the No. 3 line, said that many huggers and leaners are simply misunderstood. Mr. Medina is another kind of leaner, a bench leaner, by necessity. He is homeless and sleeps in the station. He woke up that morning on the rudely segmented bench, stretched and groaned in pain.

"Some people need to lean, man," he said. "Some people lean because they're tired."

—ORIGINALLY PUBLISHED MAY 28, 2002

RHYME, RAIL AND A SUBWAY RAT'S TAIL

In the rush of news about fare increases and potential transit strikes, an interesting piece of news was overlooked in this space last year: the announcement of the winners of the Poetry in Motion contest, in which all New York City residents with poems in their hearts were invited to submit them last spring, for a chance at having their verses displayed in thousands of buses and subway cars.

Winners in three categories—adult, young adult and children— have now been chosen, and the first poems will begin appearing in the system this October.

Sadly, this column has learned that it was not among the contest's winners—in large part, apparently, because of a failure to mail in its entries. And so, in the spirit of what might have been, here they are in their entirety, unexpurgated. Judge for yourself. (Any resemblance to previously published poems is completely incidental.)

TO HIS COY F TRAIN
Had we but world enough, and time,
This coyness, F train, were no crime.

I would sit and wait for you
Till my fingertips turned icy blue,
And thou wouldst remain
Behind a stalled work train
Somewhere near Ditmas Ave.,
So late the conductor fain would laugh.
But at my back I always hear
The office punch-clock's whirring gears;
And yonder before me lie
So many stations, so many cries
Of, "Where's the train? We're very tired.
If it comes not soon we'll all be fired!"
(The unemployment office is a warmer wait,
But none I think desire that fate.)
Now therefore, while a youthful hue
Is upon my face like the frozen dew,
Please roll my way with newfound haste
Before another morn goes all to waste.
Though I dare not dream you fast
Won't you come, oh F train, come at last?

THE BUSKER

Once upon a midnight dreary, while I was riding, weak and
weary,
To my home in a borough far,
While I nodded, soundly napping, suddenly there came a
tapping
As of someone loudly rapping—rapping on a bongo drum in
my car!
" 'Tis not right," I muttered, " 'Tis the dead of night."
"Please, kind sir, accept this dime and play your drum some
other time."

155

And a coin I dropped into his hat that sat upon the subway floor.
"That's it?" quoth he.
Quoth I, "Only this and nothing more."
Then to my nap returning, all my soul within me burning,
Soon again I heard a tapping, way louder than before.
"Surely," said I, "this man's a loon.
And he's got to stop that racket soon.
Or I will throw him out the door.
It unnerves me to my core."
"Will you cease, sir?" quoth I.
Quoth he, grinning: "Never. Nevermore."
And so the busker, never flitting, still is sitting,
Still is sitting inside my subway train
Causing mental anguish and eardrum pain.
Each song is followed by five encores
And the busker yelling:
"Never! Never! Nevermore!"

ODE TO A SUBWAY SEAT
How do I love thee? Let me count the ways.
I love thee to the width that my rear end will fit into
And the depth that I can scoot back, wedged tight
Between the sleepy guy on my left and the sweaty guy on my
right.
I love thee to the level of every day's
Most pressing need to take a load off between
Grand Army Plaza and Times Square
I love thee dearly, as men strive to get thee before I can.
I love thee purely, as I see them smugly sitting there.
I love thee with the weariness in my weary legs
And the ache in my aching feet!—and, if God choose,
I shall but love thee better after I get a seat.

SONG OF MYSELF

(From the perspective of a veteran subway rodent)

I sing the third rail electric,

I am the poet of the track and of the tunnel,

And of the small dark place to hide

And especially of the god from above

Who just cast a fresh half-eaten Danish my way.

I have heard what the talkers were talking, the talk

Of expresses and locals,

But I do not talk of expresses or locals.

Eat and eat and eat

Always the hungry urge of my world.

Straphanger, you have given me food—therefore I give to

you . . .

. . . Well, the willies.

O unspeakable passionate love!

I am not the poet of Danish only, but of bagel, of

Twinkie and

Ho Ho and of heavenly piece of hot dog.

I am not contained between my teeth and tail.

Filthy I am and make filthy whatever I touch or

Am touch'd from.

At home behind the big trash can at Canal Street.

At home next to the token booth at Tremont Avenue.

At home under the platform at Parsons Boulevard.

I know I am deathless,

I know this orbit of mine cannot be swept by a track

cleaner.

I am around, tenacious, acquisitive, tireless and cannot be scared

away.

—ORIGINALLY PUBLISHED JANUARY 7, 2003

TRAIN OF LOVE

"He lost her in the subway, down at the City Hall.
He married her that morning. That night he had no bride at all.
Just think of his dilemma. No honeymoon that day.
Oh me, oh my. I could cry. He lost her in the old subway."

—from "He Lost Her In the Subway,"
recorded by Ada Jones for Edison Records, 1907

Only a few years after the Interborough Rapid Transit system opened in 1904, it had already become so crowded and chaotic that popular songwriters of the day found the thought of losing one's bride in the subway a very funny conceit.

What follows, almost a century later, is a story with an even funnier conceit: finding one's bride in the subway.

Be forewarned: The plotline of this story is not linear. It involves, among other things, shyness, attempted suicide, panic and service disruptions before somehow arriving at its very happy ending.

The tale begins about three years ago, not at City Hall but at the 23rd Street station on the F line, where a very friendly-looking young trademark lawyer named Brendan McFeely boarded the train every morning. On a few of those mornings, he noticed another commuter—"very, very cute"—who seemed to take the train around the same time. But he could never summon the courage to talk to her.

"It just seemed too goofy," he explained. "It was the subway."

The object of his affection, Bonnie Andersen, a project manager for a real estate company, admitted that she had never even noticed Mr. McFeely, but she defended this oversight. "I'm a little cranky before I have my coffee," she said. "So I'm not really scoping people out."

Their fates could have diverged like two passing express trains. But one morning in December 1999, something happened, at once horrible and providential, to change that. Ms. Andersen was standing near the back of the uptown platform where trains enter. Near her was a man who paced nervously.

"He didn't look dangerous," she recalled, "but he just wasn't somebody that you wanted to stand next to." Her fears were confirmed when the next train roared into the station and the man leaped right in front of it.

To this day, Ms. Andersen's memories of what happened next remain hazy.

"I remember standing back against the wall going, 'Oh my God! Oh my God! He jumped! He jumped!'" She also remembers people in the train staring wildly at her through the windows, unaware that a man lay on the tracks beneath them, not dead but gravely injured. (She later learned that the man, somehow, survived.)

The next thing Ms. Andersen recalls is the complete stranger on the platform who rushed up to comfort her, asking her if she was O.K. and volunteering to stay with her until the police arrived. "He was just standing there," she remembered of Mr. McFeely. "He was the only one."

She added, "I don't know why, but I immediately trusted him."

That morning, Mr. McFeely stayed with Ms. Andersen for more than an hour, accompanying her on the subway and making sure that she reached her office. He guessed correctly that she was in no mood to be picked up right about then, but he simply could not leave her without leaving a hint. So he gave her his card.

Again, though, they almost missed their connection: Ms. Andersen was already dating someone seriously.

But for some reason, she said, she could not bring herself to throw out the business card, and when she broke up with her boyfriend the next summer, she began to wonder about the man she never saw again, the kind, redheaded one whom she had come to call "subway guy."

"I'd tell my friends, 'Someday I'm going to call subway guy,' " Ms. Andersen said. "And they'd say, 'Call him! Call subway guy!' "

So she did.

And thus on Saturday evening, slightly behind schedule—somehow appropriate given the place they met—subway guy and cute girl stood at the elegant altar of the Marble Collegiate Church on Fifth Avenue and 29th Street, he in white tie and she in a lovely white dress.

At "for better or worse," Ms. Andersen became so overcome with emotion that she began to cry, and Mr. McFeely again came to her aid, wiping a tear from her right cheek. At 5:43 p.m. they became husband and wife, kissing so ardently that the two hundred guests broke into applause.

The new couple said they had absolutely no desire to take the subway to their reception, but they did want to take a few pictures down in the place where it all began. So they hopped into a cab and shot over to the 23rd Street station.

As they walked down the platform, the train of Mrs. McFeely's dress sweeping elegantly behind her, a homeless man looked on with perplexed awe, knowing that he was witnessing a momentous occasion but having trouble figuring out just what kind.

Finally, a smile crept across his face. "Happy birthday!" he exclaimed. "Happy birthday!"

Asking a passerby for a dollar, he confided, "I just love birthdays."

—ORIGINALLY PUBLISHED JANUARY 28, 2003

TOKEN SUCKERS

In five days, when the last New York City subway token slides through the slot of the last booth to sell them, few people will notice and fewer will care. There will be no official ceremony to mark the passing. If there is music in the background, it will not be taps; it will be the bleating love song that turnstiles sing to valid MetroCards.

But off in a corner, in the shadows where things begin to smell, at least a few observers will notice and care quite a lot. They belong to a sad and desperate breed of criminal that has been in decline for a long time, one that will soon become as irrelevant to major law-breaking as moonshiners and horse thieves.

Officially, the crime is classified as theft of Transit Authority property. But among transit police officers it is more accurately and less delicately known as token sucking. Unfortunately for everyone involved, it is exactly what it sounds like.

The criminal carefully jams the token slot with a matchbook or a gum wrapper and waits for a would-be rider to plunk a token down. The token plunker bangs against the locked turnstile and walks away in frustration. Then from the shadows, the token sucker appears like a vampire, quickly sealing his lips over the token slot, inhaling powerfully and producing his prize: a $1.50 token, hard-earned and obviously very badly needed.

Even among officers who had seen it all, it was widely considered the most disgusting nonviolent crime ever to visit the subway.

"It gave you the willies," said Brendan J. McGarry, a veteran transit police officer. "We've had cases every so often, these guys would end up choking and swallowing the tokens. Then what do you do? You've got to wait for the evidence to come out."

In truth, most token suckers usually had enough evidence already in their pockets to warrant locking them up—some of the most dedicated were able to extract more than $50 worth of tokens a day. And deterrence, when dealing with someone willing to clamp his mouth to one of the most public surfaces in all of New York City, was next to impossible.

"These guys were on their last legs," Officer McGarry said. "If they were going to jail, it was just an inconvenience for them." (In an interview with a reporter for The Los Angeles Times in the early 1990's, one token sucker acknowledged the depths of his desperation. "Hard times makes you do it," he explained, adding, "Anyways, I've kissed women that's worse.")

Eddie Cassar, a retired transit officer, recalled making his first token-sucker arrests in the late 1970's, and by the time he retired in 1982, there was already a dedicated corps of inhalers, mostly teenagers and homeless men, working the station at 42nd Street and Eighth Avenue. By 1989, with the rise of the crack trade, token sucking reached almost unbelievable proportions.

During a typical summer week, repair crews were sent on 1,779 calls to fix turnstiles in a system that had 2,897 turnstiles in all. More than 60 percent of the calls involved paper stuffed into the token slots. (A related subway crime involved people who disabled the turnstiles and charged riders cut-rate fees to enter through the metal gates, to which they had stolen keys. These criminals, somewhat higher on the social ladder than token suckers, were known as trolls.)

Occasionally, methods other than incarceration were employed to dissuade the suckers. Token booth clerks were known to sprinkle chili powder into the token slots that were most often jammed. Some officers resorted to spraying a small amount of Mace around the regular slots and keeping an eye out for the usual suspects. The ones with the bright red lips were arrested.

By the time the MetroCard was introduced in the mid-1990's, token suckers could already sense the beginning of the end. But Officer McGarry said that even the introduction of advanced new turnstiles did little more than thin their ranks. By the late 1990's, he said, he was on a first-name basis with many of the sad token-sucking holdouts, who would probably never adapt to MetroCard crimes.

"It was almost like having some kind of rapport with these

guys," he said. There was one tall, thin homeless man, he said, who was even pleasant about the whole process. "He'd say, 'Hi, Mac,' when I caught him. And I'd say 'Hi' back, and he'd just walk up to me like a poodle, and I'd tell him to turn around and put his arms behind his back."

Lately, Officer McGarry said, he spots only three old-time token suckers around the Midtown area and only one who is still known to be at it occasionally. But he can't even remember the last time he locked the man up. In the end, he said, technology may have killed the token sucker. But the crime did a pretty good job all by itself.

"These guys had a lot of various diseases," he said. "You name it, they had it. You don't last too long in that line of work."

—ORIGINALLY PUBLISHED APRIL 8, 2003

SO NEAR

Before Yankee Stadium underwent an extensive renovation in the mid-1970's, a big baseball fan with small resources could take the No. 4 train to 161st Street, walk out to one end of the elevated platform and, with no ticket purchased other than a token, gaze down onto a slice of the emerald green field where legends were at play.

But then, in a serious setback for freeloading, the outfield wall was raised. Subway platform spectators are now allowed nothing more than a tantalizing view of the upper deck in the far distance, the tiptop of the stadium flagpole with its yardarm shaped like a baseball bat, and the silvery lights reflecting back out of a stadium they cannot see into.

And so the subway crowd that once gathered on the platform for games has nearly disappeared. But with the city in the throes of the first Subway Series since 1956, there are once again at least a handful of ticketless fans who believe that it is not enough to watch the game on television or listen to it on the radio.

They want to be there, to hear "The Star-Spangled Banner" echoing into the night, to hear the names of the batters somberly intoned by Bob Sheppard, the Yankees' announcer, and to try to divine from the roars and silences of the crowd what is going on behind that impervious beige wall that is about as far away as a throw to first base.

"I always like to stand here for a while, just to get the feel of the game," said Jose Esquilin, 57, a retired hospital maintenance worker. Mr. Esquilin had walked about 20 minutes from his apartment to the elevated station last night, arriving just in time to hear the Ocean Township and Point Pleasant Boro high school bands run through a blaring rendition of "Louie, Louie" one last time before marching into the stadium.

"Maybe some people feel bad, standing here so close and not getting to see anything," Mr. Esquilin said. "But it's the scene, you know. I mean, look around you. Have you ever seen anything like this? I'm probably going to go on down to Manhattan later to watch the rest of the game with a friend of mine. But you've got to come by here for a little while, right? It's the patriotic thing to do."

As Game 2 got under way last night, and a biting October wind picked up, only the hardiest of the platform fans remained, and the crowd dwindled slowly with each passing No. 4 train.

But there were still the left-out spectators who really had no choice but to stay and try to imagine what was going on behind the wall: the police officers who patrolled the platform, the supervisors who kept the trains rolling and the troops of weary transit workers who were already beginning in earnest to clean up after the crowd.

"The Yankees just scored," announced Glen Shadrick, a train service supervisor, who had cocked his ear to the crowd noise and divined immediately what it meant. Then, like an experienced platform fan, he listened for what came out of the stadium next as confirmation.

"There it is," he said. "You can tell they scored because they wouldn't play that kind of happy music at Yankee Stadium if the Mets had scored, would they?"

About 8:30, Martin Terrizzi, another train supervisor, jogged up to the platform and yelled at Mr. Shadrick, "Hey, you see that thing with *Piazza*? Oh, my *God*!"

Mr. Shadrick shot a look out from beneath the brim of his tall black hat. "Now how am I going to have seen what happened with Piazza? How did you see what happened with Piazza?"

Mr. Terrizzi admitted, "I was downstairs in the office. I saw it on television."

—ORIGINALLY PUBLISHED OCTOBER 23, 2000

THE MILK RUN

A 35-year-old man was sitting on the E train early yesterday morning, looking at the stock tables from the financial section of USA Today.

This fact may not seem particularly noteworthy. People in New York read newspapers on subways in the early morning every day.

But in this case, it was extraordinarily early in the morning: 3:30. And the newspaper was a month old. It had been folded so many times it was crumbling like dead leaves in the man's hands. The man himself was bundled up in a torn felt coat, with multiple layers of clothing visible beneath the coat. From beneath the coat, two thin legs stuck out, covered in jeans that were once blue but had taken on a dirt-brown sheen.

SUBWAYLAND

The man was sitting in a corner of the train, and above his head was an advertisement for a subway homeless outreach program, which included a picture of a homeless man who looked a lot like him. ("He May Be Without a Home, but He's Not Without Help," the ad says, showing a transit worker kneeling to talk to the homeless man.)

Asked how he had ended up like the man in the picture, the man with the newspaper, creasing it furiously, said, "I don't want to get into *that*."

In the next car, Vincent McFarland, 43, was more forthcoming about how it had happened to him. "Drugs," he said, sleepily. What kinds? he was asked. "All kinds," he said.

Two cars away, a 52-year-old man who would give only his first name, Michael, said that his reasons for sleeping on the trains were less serious, but more involved. "I *do* have a mailing address," he said proudly. "And I vote." He paused and added, "Let's just say it's a roommate problem."

His new roommates, the ones spending the night on the train with him yesterday, had few things in common. But one thing they did share was a firm opinion, one they say has been held by homeless men and women for years now:

If you have to sleep on a subway, the E train is far and away the best place to do it. Or perhaps a more accurate way to phrase it would be that the E is indisputably the least undesirable place to spend the night on a moving subway train in New York City. Some homeless men, with equal measures of affection and sarcasm, call it the milk run.

"I didn't pick this train; it picked me," said one 46-year-old homeless man yesterday morning, sitting next to a tower of possessions lashed together with bungee cords. "I tried a lot of trains," he said.

In the last several months, strong anecdotal evidence from throughout the subway has suggested that the homeless population on several train lines is higher this winter than it has been in years.

The Metropolitan Transportation Authority insists that it has experienced "no appreciable increase," but many riders say that they have, and they worry about a return to the days in which subways doubled as flophouses.

"I hadn't seen anyone sleeping in the cars literally for years," said Jim Grossman, a public relations consultant who has been taking the A to work for the past 25 years. "It started getting bad around New Year's. This morning, when I went to get on the train, one car had five homeless people sleeping on it. I can't figure out what's going on."

Neither could many early commuters on the E train, as the morning crept toward dawn. In the car where the man named Michael slept, four other men were slumped over near him, riding 32 stops in one direction, 32 stops in the other, without stirring. At one point, 15 sleepers, including 3 women, were arrayed among the 10 cars, driven in by the cold rain. Some of them drove other passengers out with their smell.

One woman furtively smoked cigarettes and engaged in a running argument with herself, screaming things like, "I'm not retarded! I'm just *tired*."

The other sleepers were silent, mostly, their bags and carts gathered around them like little fortresses. The police usually leave them alone as long as they remain upright, they say, and so they fight desperately against inertia, trying not to slump down onto the invitingly empty car benches.

Some, like Mr. McFarland, who has been homeless for 11 months, seem to have perfected the technique.

"I mean, it ain't a nice place to sleep," he said. "But you train yourself. I can get a very good night's sleep."

The sleepers say they prefer the E for simple and practical reasons. First, it is one of the few lines in the city that runs completely underground. This means that when it is very cold outside, there are no elevated platforms where the bitter wind can whip into the opening car doors.

The other reason, several men said, is that the line runs only from Queens to Manhattan, through neighborhoods they consider safe, reducing the danger that they will be robbed or beaten up or bothered.

In fact, about the only thing that bothers Mr. McFarland on the E is morning commuters. By 6:30, as his car began to fill with purposeful-looking people, he stretched and gathered up his things. It was checkout time.

"It gets too crowded," he complained. "And loud."

—ORIGINALLY PUBLISHED FEBRUARY 12, 2002

THE HANDOFF

On any given weekday, there are literally hundreds of places in the subway where an amateur performer might draw a decent crowd. But among subway show-business veterans, some stages are considered much better than others.

The hierarchy goes something like this:

Any local station, but especially one outside Manhattan, is seen as the equivalent of, say, a Hula Room at a Holiday Inn on the outskirts of Des Moines. These are the sleepy stations where rookie performers cut their teeth and gauge the popularity of their material before striking out into the larger world of mass-transit entertainment.

Further up the ladder is a place like the L-train platform at Union Square. This stage could be compared to CBGB, a popular yet intimate setting where more experienced artists can develop a cult following and make a nice profit.

And then there is the big time: Times Square, the Madison Square Garden of the subway circuit.

The most popular stage there—recently reopened after going dark for several months because of construction—sits on the main level, near the escalators leading to 42nd Street. Physically, it is nothing special: a patch of gum-stained gray floor tile, a bank of fluorescent lights and a tall white column that serves as a proscenium arch. But several hundred thousand potential audience members crowd past every day, so this stage is among the most coveted in the system.

Which raises a question long pondered by this column: at such popular places, who decides who performs when?

What happens when the break-dancers, the soul singer, the guy who tangos with mannequins and the mimes who paint themselves silver all show up at once, ready, like Mickey and Judy, to put on a show? Are there backstage fistfights? Is there some kind of roving subway booking agent?

To find out, most of last Friday was spent in the cheap seats at Times Square, leaning against a column under the Roy Lichtenstein mural.

On several occasions, it had been observed that an elderly white-haired man usually played classical music on an electronic keyboard at this Times Square stage on Friday mornings and early afternoons. Sure enough, he arrived just after 9 a.m., along with a friend who helped him carry his instrument and amplifier. He explained that his technique for securing the stage was exceedingly straightforward: he simply gets there before anyone else.

The man, 72, said that his name was Eduardo Alvarado and that he was a retired symphony director from Ecuador. He prefered to be called Professor.

For two hours, the Professor hunched happily over his keyboard, his body shaped like the letter C, playing lively pieces from Beethoven, Bach and Schubert to sparse crowds.

When he left to use the bathroom, his assistant, Francisco Yapur,

43, a sometime guitar player, guarded the stage fiercely, fending off an attempted invasion by a group of break-dancers.

"How long y'all going to be here?" one dancer asked, adding, somewhat menacingly, "We don't want to disrupt you. We just want to do our thing." But Mr. Yapur indicated no willingness to yield the Professor's spot.

"He is a money machine," he said of his mentor, Mr. Alvarado, smiling as the break-dancers wandered away.

Unfortunately, the Professor's machine was not cranking out very much money that morning. Only five dollars in bills and change sat in the wicker basket in front of his Yamaha keyboard. So when he returned, he decided to jettison Beethoven in favor of a long pop medley that began with the theme from "Dr. Zhivago," then veered into Simon and Garfunkel and the theme from "Love Story," and finally ended with a rousing version of "Besame Mucho," an electronic disco beat chugging in the background.

But in the end, the results in the basket were not much better. And so at half past noon, when Steven Clark, 30, a longtime Michael Jackson impersonator and serious subway moneymaker, showed up, the Professor and his protégé were willing to negotiate.

"Want to make a deal?" Mr. Clark asked Mr. Yapur. It quickly became clear that the two men had conducted this very transaction several times before. They walked off to the side of the stage, conferred briefly, and then Mr. Clark handed Mr. Yapur a crisp $20 bill. Mr. Yapur then nodded at the Professor, and the Professor began to pack up.

The Times Square stage handoff had occurred, in an orderly and bloodless manner.

Mr. Clark, wearing the black fedora and blousy shirt of later-vintage Michael Jackson, explained the wisdom of the deal from his point of view:

"I know that $20 I gave him is going to flip over and over for me," he said. "And him?" he said, pointing to the Professor. "He ain't going to get 20 more dollars playing today. He knows it."

Mr. Clark acknowledged that there were risks involved—namely his harshest critics, the police, closing his show down early. But he accepted this risk.

"The Constitution is on my side," he said defiantly, and then added hopefully, "The policeman should understand what I'm trying to do. He's got kids to feed, too. If he wants me to go out there and sell drugs and bust somebody upside the head, then I'll do that. But I don't want to do that."

Sometimes, sadly, subway show business can be even riskier than the upstairs kind. Only an hour into Mr. Clark's show, a couple of officers brought the curtain down on him. He had barely earned back his investment.

—ORIGINALLY PUBLISHED JUNE 24, 2003

SALVATION EXPRESS

A rush-hour subway train on a Monday morning is probably the best place in New York City to watch collective avoidance hard at work.

People are trying to avoid admitting that it is Monday again, that it is rush hour again, that they are on the subway again. They are trying to avoid touching, smelling or acknowledging the existence of the strangers around them. They are trying to avoid thinking about the rest of the morning, not to mention the rest of the week.

With this in mind, it is easy to see why Frank Meyer is not the most popular guy on the train on Mondays or, actually, any other day of the week.

Mr. Meyer is a small man with a big voice, and the only reason he steps onto a subway train is to try to force everyone onboard to think about the future. But not just the rest of the week. He wants them to think about the rest of eternity. The everlasting. The great beyond. The forever and ever, amen.

"Death will reach out its hand and take you," he told a crowd of silent passengers yesterday a little after 10 a.m., as they made their way south on an A train, not thinking about their mortality.

"Hell," he added, "is a place as real as McDonald's."

Mr. Meyer, 38, got up early yesterday and did what he does about four days a week. At Columbus Circle, he met up with a group of fellow born-again Christians who, like him, take very seriously the Gospels' exhortation to tell people about Jesus.

First, Mr. Meyer said hello to his friends—Roslyn Chan Chue, 51, an administrator at a law firm; Frank Pacific, 51, a former hospital consultant; and Darnell Harris, 45, who works for New York City Transit. The four picked up the simple props they would need for their sermons—a cup of coffee, a Danish, some newspapers. They hopped on a northbound A train, spacing themselves out along the car and being careful not to make eye contact.

And then, as the train sped down the tracks, Mr. Meyer began. He started to sing "Amazing Grace." Characteristically, no one looked up at him.

Then he took a sip of his coffee and began to make a very big deal out of it. "This is *good* coffee," he said, loudly. The people near him looked up, cringed and sunk slightly into their shoulders.

He took another sip. "I don't know why but this coffee is so *good*," he said, "that when I drink it, I just *have* to sing." And then he launched into another hymn, "Blessed Assurance."

Mr. Harris, whose transit job involves collecting the paper coffee cups and other detritus that subway riders throw onto the tracks, spoke up loudly from several seats away and asked Mr. Meyer if he could have a drink of that amazing coffee, too.

Because most people sitting near the two men at that point

did not know that they knew each other, this bit of street—or sub-street—theater produced the intended effect. People surfaced from their newspapers. A few conversations fell briefly silent. The guy with the headphones who was rocking out pulled one earpiece back from his ear.

Mr. Harris took a sip of Mr. Meyer's coffee. Then another. Finally, he smiled broadly and said, "Oh, yeah! I feel it now."

The two men ran with the coffee-as-Holy-Spirit metaphor, using it from 59th Street to 125th Street to weave a complete minisermon that ranged from redemption to judgment to forgiveness to sin, including one sin that seemed to be sorely tempting Mr. Meyer yesterday with spring in the air. ("Springtime comes and the women start wearing those clothes and, boy, do these eyes want to sin," he said of himself. "There is lust in these eyes." A woman in a business suit near him rolled her eyes.)

In a subway system where passengers are constantly being offered batteries or cheap children's toys, where they are always being asked to help the homeless or some other cause, Mr. Meyer and his fellow preachers carefully plan their pitch for God.

First, they never ask for money. They ride mostly the A train because its long express run between 59th and 125th Streets allows them as much as seven or eight uninterrupted minutes to get their message across to the congregants packed into the subway pews. They also make sure to leaven their message with a little amusement.

"Jesus did miracles first and taught next," Mr. Meyer explained. "Well, we can't do miracles, so we try to catch their attention some other way."

Sometimes it works. Yesterday, two thirds of the people in one car of an A train accepted miniature copies of the Gospel of St. John. There was even a smattering of amens mixed in along with the angry I'm-trying-to-read-heres.

Many other times, however, the seed falls on some very rocky ground. Mr. Meyer cannot count the number of times he has been told to shut up or do much worse things. Once, a man tried unsuccessfully to pitch him bodily out an open door and onto the platform.

Mr. Harris also preaches in prisons, and he said that it was hard to say which congregation was more difficult, the one in the jail cell or the one in the subway car.

"Both places, it's a lot of people sitting there, not wanting to listen," he said.

"The only difference is that the guys in prison probably know they need help. The people on the subway don't."

—ORIGINALLY PUBLISHED APRIL 17, 2001

5

HELPFUL TIPS
FOR THE NON-TRAVELER

Eye of the storm: Every weekday, more than four million
riders take the subway. Sometimes, it seems as if they are
all standing right next to you.

SUBWAY SEAT SOCIOLOGY

The ethnic multiplicity of New York is a beautiful thing, for many reasons. It teaches understanding and tolerance, or at least it should. It makes for great places to eat. It is rarely ever dull.

As an added bonus, it can help you get a seat on the subway.

The strategy is one that has been used by deft subway seat-getters for as long as there have been crowded subways. You make an educated guess about who is going to leave a seat based on how the person in the seat looks, which might indicate where that person lives or works and therefore where the person will get off the train.

Of course, it's not always about ethnicity. On southbound No. 6 trains into Midtown, for example, seatless riders place their bets on anyone with a backpack and baggy pants, because those fitting that description tend to be Hunter College students who give up their seats at 68th Street.

On the N and R trains and also the Nos. 2, 3, 4 and 5, Brooklynites coming into Manhattan in the morning will try to discern who looks powerful and pinstriped enough to be disembarking at Wall Street. On southbound A trains in Washington Heights, the clue is hospital scrubs, whose wearers almost always leave warm, empty seats at 168th Street, near Columbia-Presbyterian Medical Center.

But the ethnic strategy is one of the most reliable and widely used. And as ridership continues to climb and open subway seats become more of an endangered species (the Straphangers Campaign says that at the most crowded times of the rush, only 28 percent of riders get to sit) riders' sociological radars have become finely tuned instruments.

Ernest Enriquez, 35, a computer technician, is a student of the phenomenon. He gets on the B train in the morning near Coney Island, so he rarely has trouble getting a seat. Instead, he entertains himself by watching the seat games people play.

On the B train, it mostly involves Chinese-Americans, who get on around Sunset Park, where a miniature Chinatown has grown up in the last 15 years. Many of these passengers will then get off at Grand Street in Chinatown in the morning. So as the train fills up on its way to Manhattan, Mr. Enriquez says, he watches standing riders angle for seats by positioning themselves in front of groups of seated Chinese-Americans.

"Happens every day," Mr. Enriquez says. "They're making their odds better."

Steven Roper, 20, a pharmacist's assistant, takes the F train from Bensonhurst to Jay Street in Brooklyn, where he changes to the A train to 178th Street in Manhattan. When he has trouble getting a seat on the A, he says, he banks on 59th Street and recalls a line from a John Sayles movie, "The Brother From Another Planet."

In one scene in the movie, a magician is performing card tricks on an A train. The train pulls into 59th Street. From there, it will go express to 125th Street in Harlem and then to Washington Heights. The magician says to another character: "I got another trick for you. Want to see all the white people disappear?" And as the doors open, all of them do.

"The magic trick?" says Mr. Roper, who is black. "It still works."

He adds, smiling, that whenever he takes an N train to Benson-hurst, "the same magic trick happens in reverse: all the black peo-ple get off the train in Brooklyn by 59th Street."

"It doesn't help me much," he explains matter-of-factly, "because I'm almost home by then anyway."

As the borders of New York's ethnic communities begin to blur—as more Bangladeshis move to Astoria, more white people to Harlem—the game becomes much harder to play. Even in his years of riding the A train, Mr. Roper says, betting on a white rider to vacate a seat at 59th Street has become much less of a sure thing.

But then again, in a city as complicated as New York, it has never been all that easy, for the seatless or the seated.

Take Takafumi Kunioka. He is Japanese-American. He lives in Sunset Park and rides the B train to West Fourth Street in Manhat-tan, where he transfers to the F train to go to the Parsons School of Design.

He usually gets a seat on the B. And invariably, he says, as the train doors open at Grand Street and Chinese riders begin to pour off, the weary-looking man or woman standing in front of Mr. Kunioka will register a look of anxiety, followed by one of disappointment.

"I always know what they're thinking," he said the other day, waiting for the B in Brooklyn. "They're thinking, 'Hey man, this is Chinatown. Why aren't you getting off?'"

—ORIGINALLY PUBLISHED JANUARY 16, 2001

PRE-WALKING

Maybe it happens in other cities, too. But it seems that New York offers its residents many ways to earn what could be thought of as identification cards.

Not the laminated kind, but ones much better and less tangible. Ones displayed bodily on the street or exchanged in conversation. Or just carried around confidently in your head.

What they consist of—in a place that is complicated, chaotic and crowded—is inside knowledge of how to bend the iron city to your will. Knowing, for example, that secret way of getting onto the Brooklyn-Queens Expressway without having to take Flatbush. Or, like George Costanza on "Seinfeld," knowing where all the best unlocked office-building bathrooms are.

The subway holds out unparalleled opportunities for earning true New Yorker ID cards. But the platinum card goes only to those who know how to do something that we can call, for simplicity's sake, pre-walking.

Pre-walking involves walking to the correct place on your departure platform so that when you get off the train at your destination platform you are at the correct place to zip right through the turnstile or exit you want, allowing you to avoid the crowd and to lead the charge back up into daylight. (In other words, no more trudging behind the living dead who take half an hour to climb a set of stairs.)

Pre-walking is a quintessential true New Yorker trait because it involves not only beating crowds but also beating the clock.

"I mean, you're not doing anything except standing there waiting for the train, so you might as well do the walking then," said Ann Krone, a St. Louis woman who has visited New York frequently for years and said she felt as if she had been admitted into some kind of secret society when she figured out pre-walking. "It felt like I was beating the system," she said.

Skilled pre-walkers are not hard to spot if you know what you're looking for. Take the train to Roosevelt Island, for example. Watch how people tend to pack onto the second-to-last car in the evenings and then line up near the back door long before the train arrives at the station. This is because there's only one elevator out, and only about 20 people fit into it. The rest have to wait or suffer the long, slow escalator ride to daylight.

Nirmala Narine, a personal banker, is as good a pre-walker as you could hope to find. But even she was thrown off her game going home last week because transit officials were running shorter shuttle trains to Roosevelt Island during construction. Ms. Narine was in the second-to-last car, as usual, but those in the last car were closer to the elevator and she found herself the odd woman out, waiting for the next elevator.

"The shuttle screwed me up," she said, sounding like a pro basketball player who had just missed a layup.

But it gave her time to diagram, proudly, her personal pre-walking strategy for her morning commute: Get on the train around the middle, near the escalator on the Roosevelt Island platform. This puts her out at Rockefeller Center near the right staircase to transfer quickly to a platform for an uptown B or D. When she reaches that platform, she pre-walks to a spot near a subway map stand, because she knows that spot puts her in the right place to get out at Columbus Circle near the closest staircase to her office.

Asked how long it had taken her to map all this out, she said, without missing a beat, "Maybe being late to work twice."

Other riders have even more exacting pre-walking standards. When a request for pre-walking tales was posted on the Web site of the Straphangers Campaign last week, letters poured in with accounts, including such precise specifications as "second car, third door"; exit-closing schedules; and reminders to be careful with Nos. 2 and 3 trains because they can be different lengths.

Steve Hamill, a Web and graphics designer, and his girlfriend, Michele Bonan, a tenant organizer, were among the many who reported using geographic markers to pre-walk more professionally.

"Michele gets off at Rector Street and needs to be two benches and one map in front of our Union Street station entrance to end up at the stairs," Mr. Hamill wrote. "Unfortunately, I have to be one bench and one movie poster back in order to be at the rear turnstile at the City Hall stop, where I work."

In other words, pre-walking can divide. Sometimes, however, it unites.

A rider was at the 53rd Street and Lexington Avenue station last Sunday night and pre-walked, as usual, to his spot. Just as the train doors were closing, he looked up and saw that his wife was also on the platform and had pre-walked to the same spot.

"All of a sudden," the man wrote, "it felt like our first date all over again."

—ORIGINALLY PUBLISHED JUNE 5, 2001

WHEN NATURE CALLS

Since the early 1980's, when the subway system seemed on the verge of ruin, almost everything about it has gotten better. Hundreds of miles of rusty rails have been replaced. Stations that looked like decommissioned coal mines look like stations again. Announcements have become more frequent (sometimes even intelligible!). Subway cars nearly always have lights and no longer come with "a thick layer of rectified garbage juice" applied to the floors, as Russell Baker once described them.

But sadly, at least one place in the subway has not gotten much better over the years. It is that place where you must go when you are going somewhere and realize that you have to go—really bad.

So bad, in fact, that you will squeeze past the sad, confused-looking man in the camouflage overcoat who seems to have appointed himself the palace guard at the only men's room at the

34th Street station on the Avenue of the Americas, the one without any toilet paper.

So bad that you will brave the smell inside, which is powerful enough to bring tears to the eyes of a grown man. And so bad that you are even able to ignore the message someone has scratched into the metal stall divider, announcing ominously, "I died in here."

"I've never had to go that bad," said Tony Hernandez, standing near the bathroom late last week and watching Camouflage Man shuffle in and out, his arms full of plastic bags. "Not in that one."

"I've been in other ones," he said. "But when I go in, I take a big, deep breath and then when I come out, I let it go."

Depending on the strength of your bladder, it might be wise to develop this breathing technique. While New York City Transit does not publicize the list of the 60 or so restrooms that remain open in the subway—most were in such squalid shape that they were closed by 1982—it is often possible to find them just by following your nose.

At Union Square last Friday, the door to the women's room was wide open, allowing a fermented aroma to roll out like harbor fog. With urgent need, Aleisha Johnson started to go in but retreated before she cleared the threshold. Her boyfriend, Oston Taylor, described the odor as something "like a morgue where somebody left the dead bodies out of the freezer."

At the 14th Street station on the Nos. 1, 2 and 3 lines, the men's room was behind a metal door that looked as if it had recently withstood a rocket attack. The door was padlocked, with a chain, and appeared not to have been opened since the Coolidge administration. A congenial conductor took out his pass key and unlocked it for a visitor, explaining that the restroom was last open to the public only a week ago.

But one night, someone decided to stuff newspapers and clothes into all of its facilities. The conductor opened the door and then backed up quickly, along with this reporter. Everything inside looked green.

"Whoa," the conductor said. "Lordy."

A station cleaner said that the plumbers refused to fix the situation until she mopped it up, but she was not about to mop it up until her bosses gave her "a suit."

"You know," she said. "A hazard suit. With boots and gloves and a mask."

Fezlul Khan, the manager of the newsstand nearby, said he was one of the few who still had the courage to enter the restroom, but only because he had no choice. "Lot of people going in there and doing very, very bad things," he said.

What things?

He smiled, weakly. "Oh, my friend, you know."

In a city infamous for its lack of amenities, the subway represents undoubtedly the greatest possibility for public relief, with more than 200 restrooms built into the system, most of them in the busiest stations. But cleaning them, policing them and repairing them long ago became such a headache and financial drain for the subway that their location is now a kind of dirty secret, not included on any map or Web site and known primarily by the people who seem to live in them.

Every once in a while, these people seem to resent that the bathrooms are their residence and try to demolish them.

"I'm talking sheer vandalism just for the sake of vandalism," said Brenda Sidberry, an assistant chief station officer for New York City Transit, who added that it was hard to say how many of the 60 restrooms on the open-restroom list were open at any given time and if so, in what condition.

Fixing just one broken toilet, pipes and all, she said, can cost up to $20,000. And hiring even part-time attendants costs much more, so the idea was dropped years ago.

Last Friday, camouflage man was doing his part to help out, serving as a stable presence at the 34th Street restroom. At about 11 a.m., he settled into a stall, bags and all, and was still there an hour later.

Bob Lovett, a dancer from Naples, Fla., dozing on a nearby bench, shrugged and said, "I'm sure he's just in there installing some toilet paper."

—ORIGINALLY PUBLISHED JUNE 11, 2002

LIGHT AT THE TOP OF THE STAIRS

Nonverbal communication has always been widespread in the subway.

There are countless varieties using the eyes alone: the eye roll, the leer, the leave-me-alone stare, the suspicious sidelong glance, and the squinting of the eyelids—the universal symbol of trying and failing to understand that purling sound coming from the public address system.

There is also a clearly enunciated body language. The aggressive elbow bend, which means, "Back up off me." The kick in the back of the heel, for those who wander obliviously in front of you and cut you off. And of course, the satisfying shoulder check, deployed against egregious door blockers. (The all-purpose use of a certain finger, frequent among New York drivers, is rarely seen in such close quarters as the subway.)

But in addition to informal communication, those who run the subway have purposely created unwritten markers to try to ease travelers through the transit maze. Probably the most important and recognizable among these is the subway globe, the colored glass lamps perched atop the metal newel posts at most subway entrances. The globes are always the first interaction that riders have with the system, sometimes a block or more before they even enter it. The globes are part of the permanent street furniture of New York City and are supposed to serve as a kind of beacon, announcing that the subway system is intelligible, that people are in charge down there, and that they have, in the comforting words of Tom Bodett, left a light on for you.

But understanding the meaning of that light, and why it is a different color from the light on the other entrance, even though the entrances seem to be exactly the same, is another matter altogether.

While New York City Transit has made huge advances in the last few years in the art of speaking more clearly to huge numbers of harried people—polishing its Web site and ungurgling many of its loudspeakers—the globes endure as one of the city's largely untranslated hieroglyphs.

"They're kind of like a vestigial organ, left over from another century," said Sue London yesterday, looking up at a dusty red one in Times Square.

Though it might seem as if they have been around that long, the globes have been confusing people only for about 20 years. Before that, most lights were sheathed in milky white globes, and their purpose was illumination, not information.

But in the early 1980's, mostly to try to prevent muggings, transit officials started a color-coding system to warn riders away from entrances that were closed at night. The original idea was to follow the three-color stoplight scheme: green meant that a station had a token booth that never closed; yellow meant a part-time token booth (but in some places, with a token, you could still get in through a full-body turnstile); and red meant an entrance with no booth and no way to get in (though you might be able to get out, through one-way full-body turnstiles).

As the number of words in the above description indicates,

however, this system was much, much more complicated than go, slow down, stop.

So the yellow lights were discontinued a decade ago to simplify things, transit officials said, meaning that the red lights would serve the yellow lights' purpose, as well as the purpose that the red light used to serve. But then the MetroCard was introduced in 1994, meaning that many entrances that had been exit-only were equipped with full-body card-entrance turnstiles.

And then, responding to concerns that the colored lights did not give off enough light, transit officials several years ago began installing what they call "half-moons" when station entrances were rebuilt. These are globes that have a colored top half and a milky white bottom.

Junior Torres, smoking a cigarette yesterday near an entrance to the A line on Eighth Avenue and 15th Street, said confidently that he knew exactly what all the globes meant: green means always open, red means always closed, half-green means open most of the time and half-red means closed most of the time. "That's what they mean," Mr. Torres said, though it is not what they mean at all.

Two transit workers near a 14th Street entrance allowed that they had never known just what the colors meant. And Toribio Nunez, coming out of the entrance, said he had always assumed that they were purely decorative, like lights on a Christmas tree. "I've never looked at them, to tell you the truth," he said.

Linda Vaccari and Laura Cugini, tourists from Bologna, Italy, said they were pretty sure that the colors showed the colors of the train lines below, though, strangely, this often left them lost.

"At the beginning," said Ms. Cugini, laughing, "we are very confused."

So are many others, and not just at the beginning.

"The joke going around when these things were first installed," said Larry Furlong, an amateur subway historian, "was that green meant go in, red meant don't."

"And yellow meant take a cab."

—ORIGINALLY PUBLISHED AUGUST 13, 2002

THE SINGLES CAR

It would have taken a great deal of poetic license last Friday night to describe the first car of the Manhattan-bound F train as a happening place, the place to meet that special someone.

Just after 7, as the car rumbled out of the 15th Street station in Brooklyn, there were exactly eight people aboard. Among them was a big man in a tropical shirt with a long white beard, looking something like Santa Claus in a Jimmy Buffett suit. Across the aisle was a little boy with his head in his mother's lap, and a few seats away a man snored, annoying an already annoyed-looking girl in a torn Smiths T-shirt.

Apparently, these people had not received the official notification, the one sent out by e-mail nearly a month ago now:

"As of today, Wednesday, August 14," it read, "the first car of every subway train running in New York City's five boroughs is hereby declared THE SINGLES CAR: A free zone for unattached New Yorkers to meet the commuter of their dreams. Please ride accordingly, and work that $1.50!"

True, this declaration was issued with no more authority than you would have if you declared that the first car of your morning train was henceforth your own private hospitality suite.

True, the declaration was made not by New York City Transit or anyone official but by a group no one had ever heard of, a vaguely utopian-sounding collective with a British spelling, the Organisation for Better Underground Living.

And true, the only three members of this group—a 31-year-old

Manhattan graduate student, Christine Prentice; a 28-year-old Brooklyn architect, Marshall Brown; and a 31-year-old Brooklyn writer and editor, Mark Schwartz—had convened its first and only meeting last month while drinking together in a Park Slope bar.

But in a world where perception can drive reality as surely as the motorman drives the F train, the declaration—sent to about 250 friends and colleagues of the three—seems to be acquiring a strange kind of legitimacy based solely on the fact that someone thought to declare it.

Over the last three weeks, the threesome have been interviewed everywhere from CNN to Newsweek. And their oddly romantic idea seems to be picking up speed internationally as well, with reporters from Ottawa and Dutch television tracking them down.

"It was like, we sent this kind of funny e-mail out to a bunch of our friends," Mr. Schwartz said. "And then a week later, it's on Fox. I mean, how strange is that?"

Without seeking it or even wanting it much, the three friends are getting the kind of attention that some people pay public relations experts vast sums of money to try to get. And all for a simple idea that Ms. Prentice hoped would maybe land her a date and, in the process, remind people not to lose the kind of openness that suffused the city after September 11.

"It seemed that by Christmas, a lot of that was going away," she said. "It was really making me sad."

The fact that lots of people have heard about the singles car makes her very happy. But what would make her and Mr. Brown and Mr. Schwartz immeasurably more happy is if the idea would actually start filling the front cars of trains with lots and lots of great-looking, friendly men and women who would walk up to them and smile and say the secret password that they suggested for the single straphanger in the know:

"Excuse me, is this train going *downtown*?"

SUBWAYLAND

Last Friday, on the F line, this was not happening, exactly.

Ms. Prentice and Mr. Brown were aboard as anonymous investigators, looking around the front car, hopefully, as the train made its way from the East Village to Park Slope, territory that should have been prime recruiting ground for the Organisation for Better Underground Living.

Mr. Brown spotted two blond women in short black skirts and long black eyelashes who seemed to be on their way to a party. Could it be that the party was the one they had hoped to find here, in the singles car?

If so, it was hard to tell. The two women did not ask anyone if the train was headed downtown—wink, wink—and they sashayed off at Jay Street in Brooklyn without so much as a smile in anyone's direction.

But Mr. Brown's hopes seemed as high as ever. As the train ascended the elevated tracks in Carroll Gardens and the setting sun streamed into the car, he looked out over the Hudson and saw the Statue of Liberty silhouetted against the horizon.

"Now this is romance," he said, mostly seriously. "This is the moment when you strike."

As the train headed back into Manhattan with the snorer and the Santa Claus and the sleeping boy aboard, Mr. Brown admitted, "I guess we're still sort of waiting for our watershed moment."

Ms. Prentice helped him to define this. "The watershed moment is going to be when I meet someone on the train that I want to go out on a date with," she said. "That's when it's going to be."

—ORIGINALLY PUBLISHED SEPTEMBER 10, 2002

WAITING ON A TRAIN

If you are standing on a subway platform in London or Barcelona or Washington and wondering when the next train will arrive, there is generally no great effort involved in finding out: look up at the colorful screens, the ones that want you to have a nice day, and watch as the electronic seconds count down to your ride.

In New York, characteristically, much more talent is required.

The most popular methods are, of course, the platform lean and the long tunnel stare, timeless images of urban impatience.

Experienced commuters usually combine the stare with a subway distance technique that may have some relation to the sonar used by bats and which can help predict the proximity of the train simply from the size of its distant headlights.

And true veterans take into account even more esoteric signs—the metallic pings of the tracks, the fetid breezes and the scurrying mice, which are the canaries of the mass-transit coal mine. In the end, though, even the most talented train spotter can misread these signs and watch sadly along the local track as an express blows by.

So now, as New York City Transit draws up a new contract and prepares yet again to find a company to tow it into the electronic information age, there is hope that—finally, this time—these subway tracking skills will be rendered vestigial.

For more than a decade, the agency has been trying to join its more technologically advanced counterparts and install a computer system that will allow train dispatchers to know something that most riders might be disturbed to learn the dispatchers do not already know: exactly where the trains are.

In many ways, the system still works much as it did when the subway opened: the wheels and axles of the trains cause a short circuit along a section of running rail, illuminating a little red light on a big black map in a tiny room deep within the heart of the subway.

This tells dispatchers where a train is, sort of, but not which train it is, exactly.

In fact, the train is positively identified only when it comes into the station and subway workers lay eyes on it and jot down its car numbers on a handwritten sheet. A train supervisor once described this system as "kind of like watching the minute hand on a clock."

"It doesn't give you a lot of details," he said.

If the professionals do not have the details, they cannot very well pass them on to the passengers, and so far the agency has had huge trouble—partly through its own oversights, critics say—in finding a company to help it build a system to collect those details.

Its first effort to put passenger information screens into the system envisioned them being in 137 of the system's 468 stations. It ended up putting them in only 51. And most of those screens are not tied into a central computer, meaning that they are sometimes manually operated and of little use in delivering accurate, real-time train information.

"It usually is just a generic message that says 'It's pickpocket season!' or 'Have a nice day!' or 'Yada, yada, yada,'" said Paul Fleuranges, a spokesman for the agency. Karl Steel, an official in charge of finding a better system, added yesterday, "One of the lessons we learned is that if you're giving wrong information, then sometimes it's better not to do it at all."

The agency insists that it does want to give the right information, however, and so it is now in the middle of a complex project to tie all the antiquated signal equipment on the numbered subway lines to a computer system that will track trains better and allow information to be passed to riders.

A second project will modernize the signal equipment on most of the lettered lines, which is so antiquated that it cannot even be tied into computers. And subsequent projects are to bring information screens on which the numbers "3 . . . 2 . . . 1" will usually coincide with a train pulling into the station.

Even with this in mind, it is probably not advisable to let your personal subway-tracking skills lapse just yet. If the projects go as planned—an "if" that grows larger with each failed effort—information signs will not start appearing until well after 2005.

Until then, officials say, they are simply working much harder to improve the old-fashioned system of telling people where their trains are—with humans like Robin Anderson, who sits in a control center at DeKalb Avenue in Brooklyn. Every morning, she and a handful of colleagues are the ones who stare at the little lights on the big maps and translate what they see over loudspeakers in 155 stations.

These days, most of those speakers do not sound quite as much like the teacher's voice in the Charlie Brown television specials as they once did. But some still do.

In those cases, it might be a good idea to learn a new subway-tracking skill, one advocated by Garrison Keillor when he lived in New York: upon entering the station he surveyed the platform and if it was full, he knew that a train was nigh.

"It always makes me feel good," he said, "knowing that some of the job of waiting has been done by other people."

—ORIGINALLY PUBLISHED OCTOBER 15, 2002

STAND CLEAR OF THE LOVE SEAT

City life, especially in New York, requires countless daily calculations involving the fundamentals of physics: space, time, mass and energy.

Can I really fit this couch into my apartment and still have enough room to live in it? Can I actually make it across six lanes of traffic on a blinking "Don't Walk"? Can I legally put a broken

27-inch television, an old microwave and an entire set of barbells into the recycling? Can I possibly remain conscious for eight hours today after sleeping only three last night?

Then there is the thorny question combining all of these elements, the one that requires the most advanced form of urban reckoning:

Can I carry it on the subway?

It is not a problem unique to this city, but it is certainly confronted here more than anywhere else in the country. Even in other cities with mass transportation, car ownership has remained high, but New York has long been an exception. According to the 2000 census, 54 percent of city households do not own or lease a car. In Manhattan, in fact, 78 percent remain carless, a virtual republic of unrepentant pedestrians.

In other words—while deliverymen and cab drivers sometimes fill the role here—the subway is this city's communal station wagon, a freight train in all but name. While other Americans may arrange their purchases neatly in capacious car trunks, New Yorkers are towing theirs mightily through the turnstiles. While other Americans may strap surfboards atop PT Cruisers, New Yorkers are dragging theirs onto the A train to Far Rockaway.

And while other Americans try to lock in a good radio station on the highway, New Yorkers are trying to figure out how to hang onto the pole in a packed train without losing control of the briefcase, the overcoat, the gym shoes, the large box of Pampers and the Big Brown Bag from Bloomingdale's.

This dilemma—balance versus baggage—has confronted subway riders virtually from the start. In late November 1905, only a year after the subway opened, The New York Times published an account of a man carrying a suspiciously large parcel wrapped in yellow paper, which fell from his arms at 72nd Street. "The crumpled top opened," the story said, "and after a few kicks and flurries, a turkey, with an air of outraged dignity, strutted out on the floor."

Over the last two years, in an attempt to document the phenomenon, this columnist has kept a sporadic list of the most unwieldy cargo spotted aboard subway cars. If nothing else, it shows what human willpower can still accomplish without internal combustion—in fact, with little more than a MetroCard and a strong back.

Among the entries are these:

- November 2000—A man with a dolly wheels a mahogany-brown, four-drawer dresser onto the A train at Times Square. Riders comment on how nice it is. (The dresser, not the train.)
- December 2001—A man on an N train in Sunset Park is seated, with a recently purchased Christmas tree at least eight feet tall clamped between his legs. Behind the tree he is reading a book.
- September 2002—A man and his girlfriend carry a sousaphone onto a Q train in Midtown. He carries the body around his shoulders while she holds the brass bell on her lap. A woman sitting next to them, apparently not a music lover, looks very angry.

Correspondents have also helped in this documentation, sending in their own strange cargo sightings and experiences. For example, a newspaper reporter's wife told of how she carried a nine-foot whaler's harpoon, a gift for her husband, on the train. The only real difficulty involved jamming the harpoon through the bars of a full-body turnstile, much the way that Captain Ahab might have jammed one into the ribs of the great whale. Unlike Ahab, she had some luck and caught the next train.

Users of the Straphangers Campaign Web site submitted a

subway cargo manifest that included a television, a huge decorated pumpkin, an office chair, a double stroller with a home entertainment system balanced on it and an entire love seat ("Guy had a couch in the middle of the subway car and was just relaxing as if this was not at all strange," one rider wrote).

If there were awards for subway portage, Michael Hernandez, a field organizer for the campaign, would undoubtedly be among the winners. He has taken a mini-refrigerator aboard the train, he said, and he once managed to get a four-foot houseplant home that way, alive.

But even he admitted that he made significant errors in his urban physics when he decided to carry on a 10-foot-tall disassembled closet that he had bought at Ikea in Elizabeth, N.J., and brought back into the Port Authority terminal on the store's free bus.

"I guess I didn't put enough thought into it," Mr. Hernandez said recently. "I was, of course, smacking it into people. It was way too heavy, taking up way too much space."

He added, soberly, "It's something I don't ever want to do again."

—ORIGINALLY PUBLISHED OCTOBER 29, 2002

SUBWAY LULLABY

It is hard to imagine a place less conducive to slumber: a rigid plastic seat beneath harsh fluorescent lights in a crowded, narrow, metal room that lurches and lists. Every few minutes the doors open, a two-tone alarm rings out, and a stranger announces instructions over a loudspeaker. The room, meanwhile, is filled with dozens of other people, including several crying babies, a bongo player and maybe the mayor of New York City, holding an early morning meeting with his staff about new taxes.

In many places, such a room might be described as a sleep

deprivation chamber, like the ones used in the late 1950's to determine whether prospective astronauts had the right stuff.

In New York City, such a room is known as a subway car, a pretty great place for a nap.

"For me," said Ginia Guzman, waking reluctantly on the downtown Q train yesterday morning, "it is the best place."

Ms. Guzman lives in Flushing and works as a housekeeper in Flatbush, Brooklyn. While her subway trip between those distant points might not always be reliable or pleasant, she can always count on one nice thing en route. "I sleep like a baby," she said, rubbing her eyes as the train emerged into daylight on the Manhattan Bridge.

Of course, if she had a choice she would naturally pick a more comfortable place to snooze—a couch, say, or a chair in a quiet room. But she lives in the city that never sleeps. Or, more accurately, the city that never sleeps when it is supposed to and certainly cannot catch up while cleaning a house in Flatbush.

So Ms. Guzman positions herself at the end of a subway car bench, loops the strap of her bag protectively around her arm, tucks her chin into her chest and makes do. The subway may be lacking many things, but a certain kind of solitude is not one of them.

Until yesterday, when a reporter gently woke her to inquire about her nap, no one else had ever bothered her while she slept, and she said she tended to sleep quite soundly.

"After a while," she explained, "you get good at it."

The art of the New York City subway nap—polished and perfected by everyone from stockbrokers to street messengers, often side by side—is actually a more recent phenomenon than most people realize. In the early days of the subway, the police regularly roused sleepers, relying on a section of the old state penal code that prohibited sleeping in public transit areas.

In 1953, there was a fleeting moment of hope for nappers when

City Magistrate J. Irwin Shapiro dismissed charges against some subway-car sleepers, declaring them to be "human souls whose rights may not be trampled upon" and admitting that he had dozed off on the subway himself.

But then the police began charging sleepers, somewhat paradoxically, with disorderly conduct. And when the penal code was rewritten in the 1970's, sleeping was generally lumped into the category of criminal loitering. So the golden era of unfettered subway napping did not really begin until 1987, when an appellate court ruled that arresting people for loitering in public transit areas was unconstitutional.

Of course, the ruling mainly concerned homeless people who sought out the subway for much greater necessities than sleep, such as warmth and shelter. But a side benefit was to make the casual nap perfectly legal—as long as one manages it with some skill and does not slump over onto two or more seats, a violation of a subway administrative rule.

Monday mornings are generally thick with subway sleepers, even snorers, as work rudely extracts people from their weekends. Yesterday morning did not disappoint. There was the busboy from a Greek restaurant in Astoria, who had worked a double shift and was rocking forward so wearily on the W train that his cigarettes almost spilled from his shirt pocket.

There was the guy on the uptown No. 3 train, soundly sleeping though his shiny eyes remained partly open and his teeth balanced a toothpick. "Is he dead?" a passenger asked.

There was the 45-year-old off-duty engineer for New York City Transit, who did not want to give his name because he was afraid it might seem as if he were sleeping at the office. With some authority, he declared the R to be among the best sleeping trains, because it is slow and tends to rock side to side on its tracks in Manhattan.

There was also Sharee Taylor, a 16-year-old high school senior, who slept on her way to a college fair in the Bronx. Like most experienced nappers, she has developed a kind of internal alarm clock that wakes her reliably at her stop, though she admitted, "One time I was on the way from Brooklyn to Manhattan and I woke up in Queens."

Tuvia Yamnik, a cantor, never naps, but he said he loved to watch the nappers and wonder what they were dreaming. "Life is tough," he said. "Maybe they have a fight with their husband, their wife. They dream everything is O.K."

—ORIGINALLY PUBLISHED JANUARY 14, 2003

DOWN AT THE LOST AND FOUND

Remember that night on the subway when you had a few too many and somehow lost everything you were carrying: your watch, your coat and your glasses, along with your bicycle, Bible, coffee maker, violin, VCR, power saw, pool cue, fax machine and favorite box of Statue of Liberty figurines?

If you were thinking of trying to reclaim those things, you have sadly waited too long. Yesterday morning, deep within the recesses of Pennsylvania Station, as a water cooler gurgled and trains thundered overhead, all of your possessions became the property of the highest bidder.

And in the business of redistributing the wealth that goes unclaimed in the city's vast transit system, it turns out that a high bid is a decidedly relative term.

"I have here lot No. 35," called out Cornelius A. Heaney, the hopeful auctioneer. "Eight boxes of assorted Bibles. Who will give me $40?"

Silence. Water gurgling. Trains thundering.

"With these boxes," Mr. Heaney added, doing his best W. C. Fields, "you can open your own hotel."

Silence, gurgling, thunder.

Finally, he dropped the opening bid and for a mere $20 unloaded most of the Scripture misplaced in the city's subways and buses over the past five years, since the last time New York City Transit's Lost Property Unit held an auction to try to clear its crowded shelves.

"God," Mr. Heaney complained at one point to the 52 people sitting before him, carefully biding their bid paddles. "I'm *giving* this stuff away."

For Charlotte Roseburgh, the director of the unit and the woman in charge of cataloging all the lost stuff, giving it away must have sounded like a great idea yesterday. As she describes it, the subway's lost and found is much more a place of loss than of finding.

In fact, if democracy is a form of government predicated in part on the sanctity of property, a look around the Lost Property Unit and its tens of thousands of unclaimed things can make one a little worried about the state of the nation. "I cannot understand," she said, "how someone loses a bike. Don't they miss it? Don't they need it?"

Apparently not, judging from two lots yesterday of 25 bikes, most of which were bought for $80 by Darnell Owens, an amateur comedian from the Bronx, who later spotted a couple of sad examples sitting on the auction floor and said, "I really hope mine don't look like that."

People apparently also did not miss or need their calculators (58), beepers (285), radios (59), CD players (77) or small televisions (3). Or, for that matter, their violins (5), guitars (4), clarinets (13), flutes (3), trumpets (3) or a decent marching band's worth of other instruments, including a box of tambourines and a saxophone won for $175 by Kenya Nkhrumah, who does not play the saxophone.

"My daughter does," he explained, adding that he had not seen the sax and hoped it played a little. "I went on faith," he said. "Pig in a poke."

After seeing so many odd, smelly, useless, frightening and often unclassifiable personal possessions, Ms. Roseburgh said that it was very difficult for her to name the strangest. The now-legendary prosthetic legs predated her time as the head of the office, though false teeth and bridgework still arrive occasionally. There was the man who lost a Minolta copying machine but came back for it. (People have six months to claim property before it is marked to be sold.)

Behind her on a shelf were items that even the auctioneer did not think he could sell, like a plastic hippopotamus, a windup walking eyeball, a rubber skeleton and an old book about rheumatism.

Ms. Roseburgh said that some people, out of the goodness of their hearts or the depths of their psychosis, tried from time to time to turn in items, only to be rejected. "When I was a booth clerk, I had people turn in pennies," she said. "Once, somebody turned in some yogurt."

Recently, there was a hospital vial full of a tea-colored liquid. "I don't know *what* that was," she said. "Sometimes people are just lonely, and they want to turn in something so they can have some-one to talk to."

It seemed as if a few of the bidders yesterday made their way underground with the same lonesome motives, sitting on the benches and staring ahead with strange, empty smiles. But enough serious players also arrived for the auction to be declared a qualified success by Mr. Heaney, who once auctioned off an entire subway car.

Yesterday was not nearly so glamorous, he said, but at least every-thing sold—right down to six boxes of unclaimed keys for a dollar.

One bidder, a man named Ariel with a ponytail and a chain on his wallet—no last names, please—said he was leaving quite satisfied, having won the bidding for a box of 210 metal charms and pendants at $250.

What did he plan to do with all of them? He looked at his questioner suspiciously. "That's something I really don't want to get into."

—ORIGINALLY PUBLISHED JANUARY 14, 2003

DISASTER DOWN UNDER

Destruction from above: Eight months after the World Trade Center attack, rubble remained like a tombstone at the Rector Street station.

LAST TRAIN

When Carlos Johnson woke at his usual hour—3:30 a.m.—on Tuesday, September 11, he did not know that hundreds of miles away, a 190-ton jet sat on a runway in Boston, bound for the very place he was bound that day.

He did not know, as he parked his No. 1 subway train at its terminal in the Bronx, as he took his morning break, going downstairs for a bowl of oatmeal and a slice of toast, that the jet was closing its doors, about to pull away from the gate.

And he did not know that when he rolled out of the terminal for his second trip south that day—his train designated Van Cortlandt 748, for 7:48 a.m.—that it would be the last time he would travel to the end of the 83-year-old subway tunnels that have been his office and his occupation for the past nine years.

Mr. Johnson is not a romantic about the subway. It is a job, a reliable one that has helped him and his wife, Rhonda, raise three children in Woodbridge, N.J. But as a motorman who has spent most of his career on the No. 1 line to South Ferry, which threaded him through the heart of the World Trade Center, he knew every part of the line as well as he knew his own name.

He also knew, at least by their faces, many of the people that he saw day by day flooding out of his train, up the south stairs of the Cortlandt Street station, bound for the long elevator ride up the towers.

And before he became a motorman, Mr. Johnson was a track worker who—even he finds this strange now—spent much of his time, long nights in the dust and heat, working inside tunnels of the No. 1 line in Lower Manhattan. "It seemed like fate said: 'This is your part of the subway,'" he said.

Like hundreds of thousands of people in the city, Mr. Johnson remembers events that morning with powerful clarity. He remembers that when he pulled into the Chambers Street station, one stop north of the World Trade Center, the digital clock at south end of the station clicked 8:45 as he watched.

The doors closed and he sped south. He pulled into the Cortlandt Street stop and brought the train to a halt at exactly 8:48, just as the first jet slammed into the north tower. But he still had no idea of the role he was playing in that day's events, taking one of the last trains through what would later be known as ground zero.

"People who had gotten out of the train started running back down the stairs," he recalled last Saturday, resting in Harlem after returning to work on another line. "And there were other people still trying to get up the stairs. I saw people get knocked down. "And I heard someone say: 'They're shooting upstairs! They're shooting! Someone has a gun!'"

In the list of dangerous things that Mr. Johnson has thought about encountering on his train, even a gunman seemed on the outer edge of possibility until that day. "You never imagine worse things. You worry about a derailment. Maybe a bomb in the train, but the odds of that seem so long. And so when I heard someone say that there was shooting upstairs, it seemed like a huge thing. I don't panic, but I said to my partner, the conductor, 'Let's get this train out of here.'"

He said he envisioned the gunfight spilling down onto his train. As he said this, he smiled and shook his head. "If I had only known what was really going on right over my head," he said. "I didn't hear anything. I didn't feel anything. The lights didn't even flicker."

He took his train downtown to the South Ferry station, where he finally got a supervisor on his radio and heard that it was not gunfire, but some kind of explosion. He still did not know whether to believe it. Rumors and confusion, he knew, travel down the tracks much faster than the trains.

The strangest thing he remembers now is that as he headed north again, taking his train back toward the burning tower just as another plane was minutes away from hitting the other tower, he saw no pandemonium. In fact, he picked up only a few people beneath the World Trade Center, and no one on the platform appeared panicked anymore.

"I guess it's kind of like the eye of the storm," he said. "It was almost peaceful." Mr. Johnson left the tunnels and stations behind him, heading north. And only five minutes after he pulled back into his terminal and ran to find out what had happened, he watched on television as the first tower collapsed. Then he heard word on the radio that the tunnels, like the towers, had fallen in.

"That's when it hit me," he said. "That's when it finally dawned on me that I was right in the middle of it. And right then and there, I said a prayer for all of those people I saw going up the stairs that day at Cortlandt Street. I hope every one of them made it out."

—ORIGINALLY PUBLISHED SEPTEMBER 18, 2001

HEAVY LIFT

When the words "rescue and recovery" are heard, the people who run and repair the 722 miles of the New York City subway are not the first to come to mind.

In fact, in the encomiums that have been sung about firefighters and police officers, National Guardsmen and teamsters since the work of sifting through the Trade Center wreckage began, subway workers have figured in hardly at all. Mets have not been spotted wearing New York City Transit caps during their games. And if you asked someone at a turnstile, chances are he would guess that during the last two weeks subway workers did exactly what they have always done: they made the subway run again, a miracle in itself.

They did that, of course, and, unlike firefighters and police officers, they do not grieve for missing coworkers. But consider these questions: What other group of city workers is responsible every day for knowing what to do with tons of concrete and thousands of iron beams? What other group regularly battles water that threatens to swallow up subterranean New York? Who else, unfortunately, has had years of experience with mangled wreckage and looming collapse?

Finally, who else would have been able to assemble, within a couple of hours of the two towers falling on September 11, a five-block-long convoy of every conceivable piece of heavy machinery needed for the task, from metal saws to backhoes to loaders to dump trucks to cranes?

That Tuesday, the armies of rescue workers who swarmed over the mountains of debris learned the answers to those questions quickly, as thousands of transit workers joined them in Lower Manhattan, converging from around the city and doing some of the heaviest lifting and most dangerous work in the first days.

At the same time, the transit workers—men like José DeJesus, who usually replaces subway tracks, and Daniel Ramlal, who mans a blowtorch—learned many things themselves that they did not want to know and still have trouble talking about.

They learned, within hours, for example, that there are different types of search-and-rescue dogs.

"We'd be up there, burning through metal and pulling beams away, and the dogs would start to go crazy," said Joseph Caiozzo, an assistant chief in the track division. "And you were just sure that they had found somebody. You wanted to find somebody so bad. And then a fire chief tells you that those dogs are just trained to find cadavers. Not live people."

They learned when to look away. And they learned to lower their expectations.

"Some places, it was so discouraging because you dig for three days and you don't find a desk, a shoe, a lamp, nothing," said Mr. Ramlal, who worked balanced on high debris piles, cutting through snapped I beams that took three quarters of an hour to sever with a blowtorch. "Not any sign of human life. All we saw was twisted steel. It was just like everybody had disappeared."

When he found a tiny, almost unrecognizable doll, he jumped down to pick it up, as if it were evidence of life on another planet. "I wouldn't let it go," he said. "I thought it had to mean somebody was down there."

By early Friday, September 14, as the rescue effort began to become regimented, the subway workers learned something else: that they would be replaced and that they would somehow have to find a way to reconcile themselves to their regular jobs again. It did not happen easily.

"You had to tell the guys, 'If you are not off your equipment and back at the staging area within two minutes after the whistle is blown, you are off the job,'" one supervisor said. "You had to threaten. Nobody wanted to leave."

Mr. DeJesus, a wide-shouldered man who looks as if he would normally be the life of any party, cannot talk about it without his voice breaking. He was atop a payloader, scooping up matchsticks of metal that still bore the original markings to show how far above the earth they had been suspended just hours before: "87th Fl."

"I'm just 31," he said the other day, trying to concentrate on his track job again. "I'm too young to have anything else to compare this to."

Other men who sat around talking about it last week in downtown Brooklyn were older. They had been in Vietnam. They had been among the first to venture into Union Square station in 1991, after a horrific train wreck killed five people. They had been there to pump the water out of the crater in the basement of the World Trade Center after it was bombed in 1993, killing six people.

But they, too, had nothing to compare this with. "I was away working for so long," said Arthur Bethell, a white-haired supervisor in the subway infrastructure department. "And I heard that my 5-year-old granddaughter was asking, 'Where is Papa?' All I could think of was all those other kids asking that about parents they would never see again."

—ORIGINALLY PUBLISHED SEPTEMBER 25, 2001

BACK ON BOARD

Like many others, Edward R. Levitt cannot live his life the way he used to anymore.

He used to live in Battery Park City, but that is like an armed camp. He used to work at the New York Coffee, Sugar and Cocoa Exchange at 4 World Trade Center, but that is a smoking pyre of scrap metal.

Finally, Mr. Levitt used to motor into Manhattan, every Monday morning, from his weekend home on Long Island in his shiny, V-6, 200-horsepower Chrysler Sebring convertible.

Yesterday morning was different. He came in from Northport, N.Y., where he is living until he can get back into his apartment. He punched in at his new office, a converted warehouse in Queens where traders are so cramped they must work in shifts. And to get there he took a strange, new kind of car, one he has not taken regularly in years: a subway car.

To be exact, a rusty old Redbird, on the No. 7 line that rumbles above the park-and-ride lot near Shea Stadium.

Judging by the number of cars parked there alongside his, he was not the only car lover who has been so ground down by gridlock, so riddled with restrictions and so entreated to take the train in the weeks since the World Trade Center attacks that he has finally been extracted from behind the wheel.

It is not exactly an act of civic cooperation on his part. It is not about heeding the mayor's pleas. It is about sanity. "They've got about 100 parking spaces for somewhere between 500 and 1,000 people," said Mr. Levitt, 60, a sleep-deprived sugar trader who sometimes dabbles in coffee. (He looked as if he needed some.) "And last Tuesday, trying to drive, it was so bad I just told myself, 'This is crazy. You can't do this anymore.'"

So last week, he parked and bought a MetroCard. He is on his second one. "Do they still sell tokens?" Mr. Levitt asked as he slid a MetroCard through the turnstile just before 10.

To be honest, Mr. Levitt, the president of a trading company called Emgee Commodity Corporation, is not as much of a stranger to the subway as most of his fellow traders. They are guys—it is mostly guys—who think of themselves as financial cowboys, and cowboys ride alone, in Mercedeses and Range Rovers, not in the subway with everybody else. Traders are independent and swaggering. Traders refer to things as "bad boys." (As in, "Put some cream cheese on that bad boy," instructions to a diner waitress overheard near the new commodities exchange in Long Island City.)

Asked how his coworkers used to commute to Lower Manhattan, Mr. Levitt answered as if the question were purely rhetorical: "Well, they drove."

Mr. Levitt is a little different. He grew up on the subway. His father was a subway token clerk. As a kid, he sometimes sat on his father's lap in the booth, pushing dimes through the slot, and he remembers the thrill of the Sea Beach express to Coney Island. "I used to know all the lines," he said, smiling proudly.

But he worked hard, he made money, he bought comfortable cars and, frankly, like a lot of people, he thought of the subway as a little creepy, even when it started to get less creepy.

He did not mind the Long Island Rail Road. He did not consider himself too good for mass transit. But whenever it was time to get to Yankee Stadium to enjoy his season tickets, it was always in his car.

"Late at night up there, it's kind of weird-feeling," he said. "There are lots of rats crawling around on the tracks."

Before last week, he said, he took the subway maybe once every few weeks, when he could not find a cab. But yesterday, as he held onto a pole inside a bouncing No. 7 express on his way to work, it sounded as if he had not taken it nearly that often.

"They've really done a good job with the graffiti, haven't they?" he asked, glancing around.

In a city that says its future—at least its immediate future—will have to be tied up much more closely with mass transit, maybe Mr. Levitt is the best the city can expect.

He is certainly not happy about it, but he is doing it anyway. Before work yesterday, over toast and fried eggs, he reached into his pocket and pulled out a directive from the commodities exchange to the traders. He pointed to a sentence that he considered rather amazing: "You are encouraged to take public transportation," it said. "And if not, try to carpool."

He smiled. "Look at that," he said. "First time I've ever seen that. That's something for your story."

"It's not so bad, the subway," he said, shrugging.

Then he reconsidered, like any good straphanger. "The subway would be better if I could get a seat."

—ORIGINALLY PUBLISHED OCTOBER 20, 2001

THE MAP MAN

Maps tend to be pretty static things—at least those of known lands like New York City that were long ago explored and charted and colonized with delicatessens and dry cleaners.

At this late date, the chances are slim, for example, that a mountain will be discovered in Brooklyn. In Queens, 60th Place, 60th Road, 60th Avenue and 60th Street will probably always come disturbingly close to intersecting. Manhattan will continue to look like a lopsided schooner headed down the Hudson.

All this means that mapmakers tend to be pretty sedentary types themselves. They talk about concepts like land shape and symbology and information design. They do not usually swap stories about the last map crisis.

That is, until September 11, when so many things changed, including the humble mission of at least one city mapmaking department: the one that draws the subway map.

When the World Trade Center towers collapsed, the subway map that had been preserved under glass in 468 stations and in thousands of train cars instantly became a historical document. Hundreds of feet of tunnels on the 1 and 9 line were caved in like old mine shafts, to be closed for years. The N and R lines were skewered with steel beams. Dozens of other stations nearby were too dangerous to use, for days, maybe for weeks. And in the chessboard that is the subway system, where any move necessitates a dozen more, the scramble began.

It also began in the map department, where they are not used to this sort of thing: the subway map has been redesigned only three times in the last 25 years.

It is difficult to describe this department as a department because it is, more or less, one laconic, bearded former Georgian named David Jenkins who works in downtown Brooklyn in a gray-upholstered cubicle where there are so many piles of maps that it is difficult to walk inside.

"To be filed," Mr. Jenkins said yesterday, scooping up a heavy armful of important-looking documents from a chair and dumping them on the floor.

Mr. Jenkins is a graphic designer who moved to New York in 1981 to work on things that he hoped lots of people would look at. He ended up working on one that several hundred thousand people look at intently every day.

His first job with the Transit Authority was the subway map, back in the days when it was not computerized, when he and the authority's design contractor would have to mash little lines of tape down onto plastic overlays and hope they remained stuck where the subway lines were supposed to be. ("We always swore the tape was animate. That there were little organisms in there that moved them during the night.")

Eventually, Mr. Jenkins began to oversee the more exciting, more protean bus map, leaving the subway to counterparts at the Metropolitan Transportation Authority. But when the Trade Center attack happened, Mr. Jenkins was the man who had a working version of the newest subway map on his computer that could easily be edited.

And so, for the next two weeks, he became a kind of cartographic oxymoron: the emergency mapmaker. He worked 12-hour days through the first weekend after the attacks, etching away the solid red line that ran on the 1 and 9 from Chambers Street to South Ferry, rerouting the N and R, the J and the M, and adding stations one by one as they reopened.

He had a temporary map printed quickly in black and white. And he also began posting the computerized version on the M.T.A.'s Web site, the first time the site had been used so actively to inform riders. (Peter Kalikow, the M.T.A. chairman, said that the site usually received about 200,000 hits a day and that one day, the week after the attack, it received 10 million.)

It was not a role Mr. Jenkins was accustomed to. "You just can't turn these maps on a dime," he explained yesterday, in a deliberative Southern drawl that has not been damaged by his time in New York.

But turn them on a dime is exactly what he did. One Monday, he was awakened by a phone call telling him that a new subway station had just opened. He got out of bed, found the map on a disk he had brought home and made the change. Then he e-mailed it to the M.T.A.'s webmaster and, as he put it proudly, "people saw it when they were still in their slippers."

He even resorted to last-minute map heroics. The other day, he stood in a printing shop in Greenpoint, Brooklyn, where a small emergency map was rolling off the presses. His phone rang. The Franklin Street station on the 1 and 9 line was reopening. But the map coming off the press still showed it closed, indicated in red ink.

Mr. Jenkins sprang into action, uttering, in so many words, the immortal phrase that they get to say only in the movies:

"Stop the presses!"

—ORIGINALLY PUBLISHED OCTOBER 9, 2001

SOMETHING IN THE AIR

Some people try to laugh about it, but it's not very funny anymore. "For years," wrote one subway rider, in an Internet discussion, "I had always joked that the air in the subway would overpower any bacteria/virus that could be introduced."

Others have settled into angry resignation. "I'm not crazy about being in the subway, no," said Ralph Dominguez, in the Clark Street station in Brooklyn yesterday. "But what's your employer going to do if you say, 'I don't think it's safe on the subway, so I'm not coming to work?' How else am I going to get to work?"

Others are asking themselves that question, but not rhetorically. They are trying to find new ways.

A Manhattan hospital worker is taking the bus instead of the subway, but the bus is packed—probably, she thinks, with people who have the same idea she has.

Last week, a writer drove his girlfriend to work two mornings in a row because he heard at a party that friends from Spin magazine had been told to stay away from work on Thursday, October 11, and the rumor swirled that this was because Spin had been tipped off to a smallpox attack in the subway. (A Spin spokeswoman denied this, but told reporters that the magazine was concerned about security that day, exactly one month after the Trade Center attack.)

The writer, who does not want his name printed because he still cannot decide whether he was paranoid or prudent, added, "At the time, we just thought it would be better to be safe than sorry."

Before September 11, fear seemed to be one of those things— like panhandlers or cars without heat—that was becoming more and more scarce in the new and improved subway system. Crime was down. Subway cars were crowded at 2 a.m. Tourist guides were stressing how benign the infamous subway had become. ("Statistically safer than walking the streets in daylight," one read.)

But first the attack changed that sense of security, and then the anthrax scares sweeping the city seemed to tip the scales, causing even seen-everything straphangers to start looking around, suspiciously, on their platforms.

"It makes you think about it all the time," said Mr. Dominguez, 25, a young man who doesn't usually dwell on his mortality. But right down the platform from him, at the shadowy mouth of the East River subway tunnel, he could see a police officer, Sal Menendez, standing guard to make sure that no one dashed down the tunnel with destructive intent.

There are now officers just like him at every river tunnel entrance in the city, 24 hours a day. And down inside the tunnels, says the Transit Workers Union, track workers are vigilantly looking for suspicious bags or boxes or anybody without ID pinned prominently to their uniforms.

"People don't say much to me," Officer Menendez said yesterday. "They look down, and I think they know why I'm here."

The Internet, where commuter chat rooms are humming with talk of the subway as a target, has become a kind of barometer of fear. There are discussions about how the subway is the perfect engine for a chemical attack, because the gusts of air caused by the trains would sweep substances hundreds of yards and spew them up through the grates onto the streets.

There are discussions of preparations, but not for survival. "Just make sure you have a will, designate who will care for your children, pay the insurance premiums and hope they pay off in the event of terrorism," one subway worker wrote.

There is also evidence of a level of official concern that goes well beyond party rumors and speculation. Last week, Daniel D. Hall, the deputy chief of the Metro Transit Police, responsible for the safety of the subway in the Washington, D.C., area, sent a message to a New York subway enthusiast Web site asking that a map showing a detailed track layout for the Washington Metro be removed.

"I don't think that it is appropriate to publish maps of the Washington Metro, that specifically show rail transfers and crossovers," Mr. Hall wrote.

David Pirmann, who founded the site, said he decided to comply, and the map is now gone. But he said he is sometimes as worried about overreactions as about the real dangers facing the subways.

"That map isn't anything that someone riding in the front car couldn't have drawn," he said. "I worry about people going overboard and about what fear does to us."

So, in retrospect, does the writer who drove his girlfriend to work.

"It does seem a little silly to me now," he said. "I mean, Spin's a music magazine. They know when Beastie Boys tickets are going on sale. What do they know about terrorist attacks?"

—ORIGINALLY PUBLISHED OCTOBER 16, 2001

A SIMPLE MEMO

New York City Transit puts a lot of faith in paperwork. At times, it seems to have missed the whole computer revolution, or at least mistrusted it. In fact, in a dusty file room in downtown Brooklyn, there are boxes containing minute-by-minute records of the daily movements of your subway line, going several back years—all handwritten, on paper.

But in the weeks since September 11, weeks that have generated enough paperwork to wrap every subway car like a Christmas gift, there are three pieces of paper that have survived consignment to the oblivion of a cardboard file box.

Instead, they have been copied and copied again and passed around like Soviet samizdat. They were written by a 55-year-old man named John B. McMahon, who works as a superintendent over several stations in Manhattan. The pages are dated and stamped, and start like any transit memo, heavy on military accuracy and acronyms, like "F.O." for field office.

"While at my office at 42nd Street and 6th Avenue at approximately 0900 hours," it begins, "the F.O. notified me . . ."

But as the memo continues, recounting Mr. McMahon's journey on September 11 from his office to the area around the World Trade Center, it quickly becomes apparent that it is something other than official correspondence.

It is the soliloquy of a man trying to figure out what happened to him that day. In essence, it is a memo from Mr. McMahon to himself.

That morning, he rushed downtown to get into the Cortlandt Street station on the N and R line to make sure that no passengers or transit employees remained inside the station. When he found none, he went back up onto the street and, as debris began to rain down from the fires in the towers above him, he took refuge under a glass awning in front of the Millenium Hilton Hotel.

At 9:58 a.m., he looked up.

He saw what appeared to be a ring of smoke form around the south tower.

"Except," he wrote, "that this ring was coming downward. . . ."

There was a truck parked next to him, in front of a loading bay at Cortlandt and Church Streets, and he dived between the truck and a roll-down door, grabbing onto the bottom of a wall.

Instantly, he wrote, "There was an upward, vacuum-type of air movement, followed by a 'swoosh' of air and then . . . NOTHING.

Not a sound, but pitch-darkness with a powderlike substance covering every inch of the area. It also filled my eyes, ears, face and mouth."

He struggled to breathe. He scooped ash and dust from his mouth. But as soon as he did, his mouth would fill up again. He felt other people around him, and he remembers hearing himself and the others count off, signifying that they were still alive.

"Then," he wrote, "the strangest thing happened.

"While I was facing this wall, I turned my head slightly to the left because I saw two lights that were too big to be flashlights and there were no automobiles around. Although I thought I was losing my battle to breathe, I was comforted by the lights, which gave me a sense of peace. We yelled, 'Help,' and joined hands, walking toward the lights. The more we walked, the lighter it became, until finally I saw images of cars and people."

But as he emerged from the cloud of ash, he wrote, he looked around him and realized that he was not holding anyone's hand. He was alone. He has no idea what happened to the other people. He still has no idea what the lights were or who was with him, and no idea how he found his way out of the debris.

"I'm a Catholic," Mr. McMahon said yesterday. "But I only go about once every five years. I don't know what that was that day. I don't know how to explain it.

"Somebody got me out," he said.

Mr. McMahon wrote the memo to his boss on a yellow legal pad at the end of that week, sitting in his backyard in Westbury on Long Island. When his fiancée read it, she cried.

"I wrote it," he said, "because I had to get it off my chest."

The day it happened, as Mr. McMahon recounted in the memo, he wandered until he came upon New York University Downtown Hospital, where nurses pulled him inside and checked his vital signs. He rinsed out his mouth and took a shower. Then he had his fiancée buy him some new clothes at Macy's so he could, as he wrote, "finish out my day performing my duties."

He is taking some time off now, struggling with hearing loss and problems with his right eye, which was injured by the dust. More than those ailments, he said, he is struggling with his own mind.

"When I tell my psychiatrist, I know it all sounds crazy to him, but that's the way it happened," he says.

Mr. McMahon's memo ends like thousands of others in transit offices around the city. On a line by itself are the words:

"For your information."

—ORIGINALLY PUBLISHED NOVEMBER 6, 2001

PUTTING THE PIECES BACK TOGETHER

On Thursday of next week, a bugler will play taps and mourners will carry a stretcher with a flag from the depths of the pit at ground zero. With that, the recovery will officially end and the rebuilding of a large part of an impatient city will begin.

But even more impatient than the city is the subway that moves its citizens through it.

And so, while real estate firms and victims' families and city officials await the ceremony and try to figure out what to build above the ground, a few hundred men have already been rebuilding, for more than two months now, what was below the ground and what will be there again: the No. 1 and No. 9 subway lines.

From the precipice of the pit, these workers look at first like all the rest, swarming over the scarred land in hard hats, day and night. But in a few minutes you can tell that their cranes are depositing steel, not extracting it. Their blowtorches are welding, not cutting. And the beams in their part of the pit are straight, not twisted, the first signs of order in a place that still looks like chaos.

"This place right here," said Dilip Patel, New York City Transit's construction manager for the rebuilding, "this is where the new tunnel begins."

Mr. Patel stood yesterday morning in the twilight of a tunnel mouth beneath Liberty Street, pointing down at a faint line in a concrete floor, near a dirty rubber boot and a plastic coffee lid.

On one side of the line was a piece of history, the sheared-off end of an IRT subway tunnel completed around 1918. On the other side, to the north, was the beginning of a tunnel that was built only in the last few weeks, its walls and floor finished and workers positioning the metal forms to pour its concrete roof.

When the workers are done at the end of September and trains with passengers are rumbling through the tunnels once again by November, it will be very hard to tell where old meets new, exactly where it was that 1,300 feet of subway tunnel were crushed and pierced by falling skyscrapers and then rebuilt in little more than seven months.

"This is a job that, under normal circumstances, could take two years or more," said Lawrence G. Reuter, the president of New York City Transit. "I've been in this business a long time, and I've never seen anything like what's going on down at the 1 and 9."

Neither have the tunnel workers who arrive there around the clock, passing through the throngs of ground-zero tourists on Church Street. Yesterday, taking their breaks, they could stare over the so-called bathtub wall, where below they could see all that was still left of the World Trade Center, a small ashen heap less than two stories high, tiny now amid the 16-acre expanse of the site. Near the pile, a group of 20 firefighters raked carefully through a field of debris before it was scooped away.

"It's sad, sad," Mr. Patel said. "It's not an easy job for anyone here."

Even in the brand-new tunnels, reminders of the catastrophe refuse to be completely erased. A beam from 7 World Trade Center pierced the tunnel north of Vesey Street, and try as they might, the workers said, they could not pull it from the bottom of the tunnel, where it lodged like a horrible Excalibur.

"We tried to pull it out with big wire cables, but it kept snapping the cables," said Avelino Alonso, a transit employee. "Who knows how far it went down?" So they just cut it off, leaving it buried beneath the new tunnel floor. Yesterday, workers in hip waders poured more soupy concrete on top of the beam, preparing for the tracks to come later.

"It's like 'Planet of the Apes' down here," said John Pegno, president of A. J. Pegno Construction Corp., which, along with Tully Construction, is in charge of the $1-million-per-day-project. "It's very surreal."

In places, the job still looks more like an archaeology dig than a subway rebirth. The ragged ends of the old tunnel walls can be seen, layers of rust-colored brick interspersed with concrete, the layers glued together with thick black mastic to keep water out.

And in fact, in many ways, Mr. Patel said, the new tunnels will have nothing all that new about them, except the addition of almost a century. They are based on old IRT drawings for the line, found in transit archives. Beams will still brace the tunnels every five feet, as in the old tunnels. Ties will still be made of wood. The steel, of course, will come from Pennsylvania.

"We think that they had the right idea 100 years ago," Mr. Reuter said. "We're a big fan of not fixing something that's not broken."

From the workers' point of view, however, there is a whole lot broken. And they have less than five months left to fix it. A visitor wished the general superintendent, Jan Szumanski, good luck yesterday.

He rubbed his sore left arm and nodded. "I will need it," he said.

ORIGINALLY PUBLISHED MAY 21, 2002

WELCOME BACK

Sometimes it seems as if the subway is not man-made but has been around forever, like a rock formation or a river, and so it should abide by certain steadfast natural laws. Such as:

The 1 and the 9 trains should go together, like Fred and Ginger, like bacon and eggs, and neither should ever go to Brooklyn. They should go to the South Ferry terminal, which should be too small and too curved. And when the trains arrive, they should always make a sound like a tsunami sweeping through a sheet-metal factory.

Yesterday morning, at least in the subway, it felt as if the world had been righted again.

It was a Monday at 9 o'clock. The Staten Island Ferry emptied its waves of weary-looking workers into the South Ferry terminal. They crowded, jostled and jammed their fingers into their ears as the scream of the trains returned to the tip of Manhattan.

And through it all, almost to a person, they smiled gratefully, like someone reunited with a long-lost brother.

"I never thought I'd say it," said Justin Hoyt, standing in front of the token booth as the din of wheel and rail drowned him out, "but I'm very happy to hear that sound again.

"It's an old, old sound."

For many New Yorkers, the ceremonies that marked the anniversary of the September 11 attack provided a moment to try to reconcile themselves to what had happened, to move ahead.

But in a city that has never been good at introspection, others looked in more mundane places for reassurance. They looked for their old routine, more precious to them than they had ever realized, and on the brand-new subway maps yesterday, many found it once again.

Little more than a year after an entire subway tunnel was crushed and the system shut down for the first time in decades, the map now looks almost as it did before September 11. The Cortlandt Street station on the N and R line is reopened, full once again of the oddly comforting sight of shopping bags lugged down from the Century 21 department store across the street.

The 2 and 3 trains are back on the express tracks in Manhattan. And the 1 and 9 are running, unbelievably, almost through the middle of ground zero to South Ferry again, through 1,400 feet of new subway tunnel built in six months—ahead of schedule and under budget, the first ribbon of rebirth amid the swept desolation of the World Trade Center site.

Walking into the South Ferry station yesterday morning, two women applauded before they swiped their MetroCards. A Staten Island man had his video camera to record the moment. Another, wearing a black "Got Beer?" T-shirt, said fiercely that he was proud to be a New Yorker.

Meanwhile, Samkutty Samuel, a station supervisor, stood in front of the station waving at people and announcing over and over through a bullhorn:

"Welcome back to South Ferry! Everybody smiling! Everybody happy!"

They were, and the two happiest men were not even commuters.

They were wearing hard hats and official-looking reflective vests and expressions of great professional pride.

One was Mysore L. Nagaraja, the chief engineer for New York City Transit and the man in charge of the tunnel reconstruction. The other was Jan Szumanski, the general superintendent of the project for Pegno/Tully, a contracting partnership that rebuilt the tunnel.

Mr. Szumanski said that shortly after the tunnel was completed on September 1 and the first diesel train successfully ran through to test it, he and his workers held a celebratory barbecue virtually atop the tunnel, toasting it with beer bottles.

"I think that once in your life, if you are lucky," he said, "you get to be part of something very special, and this was it for us."

He added, his voice beginning to crack, "For me, this is my repayment to America, for taking me 20 years ago from Poland, a nobody. That's how I think of it."

Mr. Szumanski, who has hypertension, put so much pressure on himself to finish the job early and well that he suffered an attack in the spring and was briefly hospitalized.

"I fell down, and so they took me to the hospital," he said yesterday, shrugging. "It was no big deal."

But he concedes that he has planned a long vacation in November in Mexico, where he feels that his chances of running into subway officials will be low.

Mr. Nagaraja, sounding almost serious, said to him, "Please bring your cell phone."

Behind them, the exodus from the ferry into the reborn subway continued, and practically the only way to tell that this Monday morning was different from any before the attack was that everyone seemed almost disturbingly pleased to be on his or her way to work.

Angela Brown, a transit worker who helped cut the ribbon when the station reopened on Sunday, reassured a visitor that this, too, would return to normal and make us all feel much better.

The terrorists, in other words, could not stop our subway, and they certainly cannot take away our right to look unhappy when we ride it.

"I give it a week," Ms. Brown said.

—ORIGINALLY PUBLISHED SEPTEMBER 17, 2002